FREEDOM

From

VIRTUAL SLAVERY

T. DOUGHERTY

© 2022 Sledge Press

First edition

ISBN-10 0-9908008-4-9 (Paperback)
ISBN-13 978-0-9908008-4-2 (Paperback)
ISBN-10 0-9908008-5-7 (ebook)
ISBN-13 978-0-9908008-5-9 (ebook)

All rights reserved. Excepting "fair use" as defined by U.S. copyright law, no part of this work may be reproduced or transmitted in any form or by any means, electronic or otherwise, without the written permission of the author.

Scripture quotations are from The ESV Bible (The Holy Bible, English Standard Version), copyright 2001 by Crossway, a publishing ministry of Good New Publishers. Used by permission. All rights reserved.

www.sledgepress.com

The true life is the life of faith.

—William Perkins (1558-1602)

To my lovely wife, Sherylyn

Special thanks to everyone who provided valuable feedback and comments: Joshua Haveman, Sherylyn Dougherty, Edward Morris, Robert Brown, Jason Long, and Marian Egan.

CONTENTS

1

PROLOGUE

We sometimes wander from the narrow path that leads to life and wind up instead on the wide road that leads to destruction.[1] Every once in a while, we make this choice willfully and knowingly, but much more often, we just lose our bearings and make a subtle turn in the wrong direction. The wide road fools us into thinking the narrow path is drab and impassable and we are better off taking a momentary detour. In our confusion, we compare the narrow walking path of patient perseverance with the wide superhighway of exotic enticements. In the split second of temptation, we contrast the somber old Christians losing their lives[2] on the narrow path with the beautiful and lively people enjoying all the thrills of the wide road. We make one or two hasty decisions and unknowingly begin a slow and quiet descent into darkness. Over time, the confusion grows as the darkness begins to overtake us. We move from tolerating some sin, to accepting it, to pursuing it religiously. It makes no difference to the wide road whether our sin is serious or subtle, conspicuous or concealed; it only cares that we continue stumbling in the darkness, like mindless zombies toward unknowing destruction.

1 "Enter by the narrow gate. For the gate is wide and the way is easy that leads to destruction, and those who enter by it are many. For the gate is narrow and the way is hard that leads to life, and those who find it are few." (Mt 7.13-14. Biblical citations are English Standard Version [ESV] unless otherwise noted.)

2 "For whoever would save his life will lose it, but whoever loses his life for my sake will find it." (Mt 16.25)

2

PREPARING FOR THE ZOMBIE APOCALYPSE

Monday, May 14th. The eve of the hallowed day. I have waited well over a year for the latest installment in the *Diablo* video game series. The game's developer has released a steady trickle of information about the game to build a frenzy of marketing momentum leading up to release. Like countless others, I have followed the unfolding of this plot with watchful diligence. I have carefully observed the signs and waited for the fullness of time to come. I have monitored the internet religiously in hopes of hearing the latest bit of development news or spotting the latest gameplay video. The game will be released on Tuesday, May 15th, midnight Pacific time, 3:00 a.m. in my time zone in the American Midwest.

The anticipation has grown uncomfortable as of late. Nearly a month ago, the game's developer opened the game for a one-day "beta" test,[3] and I was allowed to play for one whole joyous day. In retrospect, it was more like a cruel prank than anything; it was like giving a kid the greatest present ever, only to immediately snatch it away again. Some Grinch was laughing somewhere. That little taste of hacking and slashing

3 Many games now have short-term public tests prior to release to better ensure game stability, fewer technical issues, etc., upon release.

through zombies in dank, cavernous dungeons had ruined other games for me. The beta test was a sort of gateway drug; games that seemed thrilling the day before were now drab nonsense by comparison. With no other games that seem worth playing, my focus in the past month has turned entirely to planning for the release of *Diablo*. At this point, the scope of my planning has become practically exhaustive.

I have changed my exercise and eating habits and will soon change my sleep schedule. Like a true gamer, I am generally averse to exercise, but I have at least been doing stretches in anticipation of punishing my body with long hours in a zombie-like position—hunched over, arms extended to the mouse and keyboard, groaning and drooling in pure, pixelated joy. I also feel like I can get by on less sleep by cutting out some of the carbs and junk food, so I have been following that plan strictly. I figure I can live with only four hours of sleep each night for the first month at least. The lost sleep won't bother me; an endless series of objectives and rewards will keep the serotonin flowing. The learning curve will be steep and invigorating. The competition will be fierce and exciting. The virtual shopping is sure to fulfill a certain delightfully-compulsive consumerism in me.

I have also made several real-world purchases in anticipation of the game's release. There's a suitable gaming PC tucked away upstairs in the loft, but my family may occasionally need a reminder that I still exist among the living, and the kids will need supervision at times, so I bought a brand new laptop despite a tight budget. In this way, I will be able to play in their midst. The laptop will help facilitate the harmonious union of quality family time and uninterrupted zombie extermination.

Serious gamers pride themselves at being efficiency experts. We measure success in numerical, quantitative terms. Achievement is measured by "experience per hour," "gold per hour," "kills per hour," and so forth. Not only is it necessary to maximize the amount of time you're able to play, you must also make sure you are using each hour as efficiently as possible. I am a seasoned veteran when it comes to multi-tasking. The laptop is one of several strategies designed to help me meet everyone's needs while still being able to gain a level here and there; it should all run like a well-oiled machine. The game developer has allowed players to purchase and download the game in advance, so I have pre-installed it on both computers; they are each ready to go when the game servers come alive early tomorrow morning. I stand on the threshold of glory.

I have also customized both a gaming mouse and gaming controller. By installing and updating all of the appropriate drivers, I have ensured that both the mouse and the controller will be easily transferable from one computer to the other. I will be able to seamlessly transition between the two, so not a moment will be lost hacking zombies to slowly-disappearing bits. I have ergonomically reorganized my desk. I am hoping the newly arranged desk, along with the customized control schemes will help to minimize the pain in my right gaming hand and elbow, brought on by years of overuse. In the past few weeks, I have adapted to using my left hand to control my mouse at work, to save the right hand for gaming.

Over the course of many months, I have spent countless hours in preparation for release studying game mechanics. I have learned many of the mathematical equations behind the scenes that calculate the damage your character inflicts and receives from enemies based on your current level, weapon, armor, and so forth. There are detailed schematics in my brain of gold-farming strategies,[4] character builds, the gem and crafting systems, and equipment stats and customizations. I check several forums daily, and am an active participant in many of the discussions. I am practically a walking encyclopedia of *Diablo* knowledge. I have strategies and contingency strategies tucked away to ensure my long-term success in the game.

Kids have Christmas morning; I have May 15th. I have reorganized

4 Gold farming generally involves doing repetitive tasks to earn as much in-game currency as possible, in the shortest amount of time possible. In games, as in real life, it's hard to get far without any money.

my schedule, canceled appointments, and taken off work. Surprisingly enough, I am actually still married, and I have plans for my wife and kids as well. My wife has been wanting to visit her brother and sister-in-law, who live a state away and just had a baby. It would be difficult for her to take our young boys with her, so they will stay with me for several days. Travis Jr. is four and Jacob is two; this will be the longest span I've kept them both by myself. I had subtly planted the seed that the week of May 15th would probably be best, given my work schedule and all. I also suggested that, if she was going to leave the boys with helpless old Dad, I should probably take off a couple of days in advance to rest up and relax. As luck would have it, these days just happen to coincide with the release of *Diablo*.

If all goes according to plan, I will have two days without any responsibilities whatsoever, rising early and going to bed late. I could perhaps manage eighteen hours of play per day for the first two days, and my wife won't think too much of it. Out of guilt for leaving the boys with me for the rest of the week, she will probably overlook this unprecedented level of excess for a couple of days.

Even with the boys in my care, I figure sending my wife off to her brothers' will allow me to maximize playing time for the week. She will take our only car, so the boys and I will be limited to those places to which we can easily walk (keeping in mind that the two-year-old gets distracted by every passing car and has a top speed of about a half mile per hour). There is a park a block away and a gas station a block from that. They will quickly learn the routine; they will stay out of my hair 90% of the time in exchange for going to the park every day and hitting up the gas station for a neon blue slushy. I will play the laptop in their midst, just conscious enough to ensure they don't destroy our home. I should be able to get in twelve hours per day this way, which is probably more than I could manage if my wife were to be home the whole time. It is somewhat of an enigma to me personally, but she seems to value quality family time, and she seems to be of the opinion that isolated twelve-hour video game marathons do not constitute quality family time.

More than anyone could possibly realize, I have structured my life around video games. I don't think anyone really knows the full extent of it. I told my wife I bought the laptop for her. I told her I reorganized my desk just to get rid of the clutter. I told her I had been doing stretches because my back had been hurting a little. When she returns from her visit with her brother, the boys will speak only of going to the park every day. I will even take an hour to clean the house so there isn't so much as a hint of neglect or impropriety. To a certain degree, I must admit, I am leading a thinly veiled double life. I want to be perceived as a balanced, well-rounded Christian—everything in moderation and all of that. But *who I want to be perceived to be* and *who I actually am* don't precisely correspond. To bridge this unfortunate gap, at all times I spend part of my energy trying to conceal my true motives. I try to maintain a little distance between reality and perception. I am somewhat aware of the fact that I am, as James said, double-minded (Jas 1.8; 4.8).

I pretend that I'm nervous about watching the boys, but it's just showmanship. When my wife returns, I want to be able, if necessary, to throw it in her face how they were terrible for four days while she was off gallivanting and how I need some time away as a result. It's a scheme to get more time gaming. I'm not sure I will need to resort to it, but it's a back-up plan, just in case I'm desperate to squeeze a few more hours out of the day. It won't be the truth, but backed by my apparent frustration, she will buy it. In reality, I'm not nervous at all. They're both good boys and they both know their old man has limited patience for bad behavior.

In short, I have taken every step to ensure that there's not a moment lost leveling, collecting, planning, and building the ultimate character. In the end, through dauntless determination, through countless hours of play, I will be among the best, a god among mortal men. This is the culmination of thirty years of living and breathing video games.

The game servers come online at 3:00 a.m. Getting up at that hour will likely mess up my sleep regimen and mean less time in the game overall. Plus there will probably be "server issues" in those first few hours anyway, so I will miss the first moments, but I will set my alarm for 7:00 a.m., ready to put in a full day and then some. The whole of my focus at this moment rests upon *Diablo*. No others interest me; this is the One I have been waiting for.

3

STUCK IN HELL

The advent is here. Worship commences. Day one starts at 5:30 a.m., earlier than expected. I wake up—wide awake—without an alarm, and I am quickly off to a good start. I hack and slash through zombies and ghosts and witches and all manner of ungodly evildoers on my quest to destroy the legendary end boss, the "Lord of Terror" himself, the great *Diablo*. He is evil incarnate, the bane of all humanity, and I will make an end of him. The graphics are impressive, the controls responsive, the experience substantial and fulfilling. My character is level ten in a blink. I stand knee-deep in corpses with the sounds of war and the stench of blood all about me; it is everything I hoped it would be. The servers are down for a couple of hours here and there throughout the day, which is frustrating, but more or less expected for an online-only game on the first day, when millions of people are clamoring to jump on a massive cloud of servers somewhere to play for the first time.[5] I use the downtime to run to the grocery store or grab a bite to eat; I might as well get chores out of the way in order to buy myself an hour or two somewhere down the line. Even with the delays, I am still able to get in twelve hours

5 The player has to be connected to the internet to play, and the game developer hosts hundreds of servers through which each game is routed. This allows players from all over a given region to play in the same game with one another simultaneously and allows the developer to actively monitor cheating, hacking, etc.

of play. I go to bed bleary-eyed but satisfied. There is still more to come; best vacation ever.

Day two: the game is working a little better. I put in seventeen hours, stopping only for acute bladder pain or to wolf down whatever the kids didn't eat of their lunch. There's no time to stop and make something. In the quest for glory and gold, I am well ahead of the pack.

Most games today feature an eBay-style "auction house" where players can sell their unwanted game items for game gold or use their gold to buy items posted by other players. In addition to this, *Diablo* is to offer a second "real currency" auction house, where players will be able to sell game gold, as well as items found in the game, for real money. As if I needed more incentive to play video games, now there's real money at stake. I will earn a little virtual capital by playing the game as it was intended, and then try to invest that capital in the in-game auction house. Market supply and demand establish the real-world value of game gold at any given moment. Basic economics apply; buy low, sell high. Figure out a way to make a penny buying and selling swords or jewels or whatever, and then repeat it a few million times as quickly as possible.[6] It's a stock market, but more predictable; there are predictable weekly cycles of supply and demand, since more people play during nights and weekends and demand is naturally higher. There are also cycles based on the influx of players from game updates, patches, and expansions. Timing the market will be crucial. The games' creator will naturally take a sizable cut of any profits.

It was genius—what greater incentive could there be to keep us

6 Many websites popped up prior to release where players could share their ideas and theories as to how to "flip" items on the auction house to turn a profit, or how to exploit discrepancies that arose between item prices on the gold auction house and the real money auction house. For instance, you could potentially buy an item for real money, sell it for game gold, sell the game gold back for real money, and turn a profit in the end. Players even began developing software systems to look for pricing discrepancies and to monitor the market in various ways. Gamers became economists almost overnight.

all playing? It will make all other games feel shallow by comparison; it was already having that effect on me. How would I play games without real money once I had played a game *with* real money? It made all other games feel somehow less “real.” I’m not sure I could go back to the same old moneyless games at this point. Don’t get me wrong, I don’t expect to quit my day job or anything. In reality, I figure good players, selling most of their gold, will make a couple of bucks per hour, tops. They will, of course, have to sacrifice their own games to a degree, selling off their gear and items for a little bit of real cash. I would have to play twice as much to ensure that my character is solid and that I still have plenty of gold left over to sell for profit.

At the end of day two, I close my eyes to go to sleep and see endless images of shooting arrows, flailing swords, dismembering explosions, and a profusion of cartoonish gore. The sounds of warfare are unending. I have meditated intently on a screen for seventeen hours, so it’s no surprise these images are hard to shake. With only five hours of sleep planned though, I get irritated with myself that I can’t clear my mind and doze off.

Day three: the better part of my vacation is behind me. I am anxious to get upstairs to continue the annihilation of *Diablo*’s minions, but I have to help my wife out a bit this morning. She is leaving to visit her brother today, and then it will just be the boys and me for the next four days. I have the laptop; I will not neglect them, at least not in the *legal* sense of the word. Complaints of hunger will be met with food. Smelly diapers will be changed.

By 10:00 a.m., my wife is long gone, the boys are fed, and I am downstairs on the new laptop, picking up right where I left off. Not everything goes to plan though. The smaller screen makes the game harder to see, and the resolution is much lower. Plus the game runs slower overall through the Wi-Fi connection, and a wired connection is not possible. This is a chaotic game that requires quick thought and action; the small details are important. The laptop is not sufficient, and I am frustrated. I should've thought ahead! I should have been better prepared; this was a major slip up. I sit brooding and sulking for half an hour, watching all of my planning slide right down the drain.

I start to think about how the boys would do unsupervised. The real liability, I suppose, is that Travis can open a couple of exterior doors in the house, in which case his little brother Jake could escape and wander down the street. Jake did it once before, but fortunately didn't make it more than a couple of driveways away before a neighbor alerted us. We have a fearless two-year-old, and we live on the corner of two fairly busy streets. Zombie carnage was one thing; toddler pedestrian street carnage was better to be avoided. I decide a serious talk with Travis is in order. I call him over and cradle his face in my hand so he looks me in the eye and understands I am serious.

"I want you to listen to me, ok? I do not want you to open any of these doors. If you open any of these doors, you'll get a big-time spanking." I gesture as I talk. "I'm talking about this door and that door and the garage door too. You are not allowed to open any of these doors. Do you understand me?"

He concurs.

"Do you understand me?" I ask again, with increased gravity, just for good measure.

He concurs again, with seriousness sufficient to appease me.

I am upstairs in the loft. I keep the sound down so I can try to monitor the boys. When they are too quiet—generally a sign of mischief—I yell down for Travis, and when he responds I ask him what Jake is doing. I try to discourage them from going down into the basement because I won't be able to hear them. I keep the TV on in the living room; a 24-hour cartoon channel should keep them centralized there. We'll still go to the park as planned. It will make me feel like a more successful father anyway, minimizing self-doubt and maximizing pure fun. I give them a quick breakfast, lunch, and dinner whenever Travis complains about being hungry. I put Jake down for a nap at 1:00. Otherwise, I am saving the world from evil upstairs. The boys are in bed at 8:00; I am in bed at 2:00 a.m. I have beaten the game on normal difficulty; fame and riches here I come. The game is an instant hit; it sold 3.5 million units the first day, plus another 1.2 million players received the game for free as part of a promotion—the fastest-selling computer game in history.[7]

Day four: up at 7:30, I microwave the boys something for breakfast, and I am upstairs dungeon crawling, still calling down every half-hour or so, "Travis, what's Jakey doing?" I am level 45 now, out of 60.

As it turns out, "beating the game" is a meaningless concept in *Diablo*. You beat the game once and then automatically start over on a higher difficulty with tougher enemies who carry more gold and better loot. You progress through Normal, Nightmare, Hell, and Inferno difficulties. Each difficulty poses a successively greater challenge, and the game's creator wants you to run up against a wall and get stuck at some point, so you are forced to go back and replay old content. It's no secret to anyone that this is how they hope to keep players hooked indefinitely. The incentive for the player to replay old content lies in finding more gold and better items, which in turn translates into a progressively stronger character capable of making it successively deeper into the game. The ultimate goal is killing *Diablo* on inferno difficulty, but to get there you'll have to spin your wheels collecting gold and wheeling and dealing on the auction house for a very long time.

A successful economy is, therefore, crucial to the game's long term success. The game's creator has to ensure there are enough "gold sinks" (such as the cost of repairing your equipment)[8] to make sure gold

---

7 Schroeder, Stan. "*Diablo 3* is the fastest selling PC game in history." *Mashable Entertainment.* http://mashable.com/2012/05/23/diablo-3-fastest-selling/

8 When you defeat an enemy, they drop some gold, and so there is a constant influx of gold into the game. As more and more gold is generated, its value decreases, and item prices begin to go up to reflect a devalued game currency. This is inflation. To avoid inflation, game developers have to figure out ways to balance gold coming into the game with gold disappearing from the game.

is always in demand and there's never quite enough to go around. The moment a player feels he has "enough" gold, the thrill of the hunt is over, the learning curve tapers off as mastery is achieved, and he quickly loses interest. When inflation starts to occur, the game maker will tweak how much gold drops from dead zombies and such, along with 100 other factors to ensure relative and permanent economic stability. So few players have put in sixty hours in four days that I am further along than most. I am selling high level items at a premium to these lower-leveled noobs. Inferno *Diablo* will kneel before me! The boys are in bed at 8:00; I am in bed at 3:00.

Day five: up at 7:30, breakfast, play until 12:30, a quick lunch for the boys, put Jake to bed, play until 6:00., a quick dinner for the boys, park for one hour sharp, bath and bed at 8:00, play until 2:00. I beat the game on Nightmare difficulty. I have completed two of four difficulty levels and am halfway to ultimate victory.

Day six: my wife comes home today. I have to work tomorrow. I will have to allot an hour to cleaning; the place is a mess. The house will be mostly picked up, the boys will talk only of going to the park every day and glutting themselves on neon slushies, and I will likely be crowned as father of the year. There will probably be no need to complain about how difficult they were; I will play it by ear. I don't expect my wife home until 8:00 p.m. or later. I am up at 7:30, breakfast, play until 12:30, quick lunch, Jake's nap, play until 6:00, quick dinner, park for one hour sharp, clean for an hour, bath and bed at 8:00. I am on Hell difficulty. My progress in the game has screeched to a halt over the course of the day. I knew the game was structured in such a way that you're supposed to run up against a wall at some point, but still it is a strange blow to the ego. I may be no match for the Lord of Terror after all. I suppose the pain of running up against a wall is relative to the speed at which you were running at

---

In *Diablo*, you have to spend gold to repair your equipment, and you can use gold to create new items, to purchase consumable items such as potions, to revitalize your health, etc.

the time and whether or not you saw it coming just beforehand. I was blindsided; I feel anxious. Yesterday, the game was a fast-paced smash-and-grab; today it has become a slow and grinding struggle. In my mind, I envision hordes of other players, right on my tail, catching up quickly while I'm getting nowhere fast. It's important to stay ahead of the pack to maximize profits. I see online that others—a few others anyway—have beaten the hardest difficulty and I grow envious, covetous, angry.

My wife comes home later than expected, a little after midnight. She catches me up on how her trip went. My mind is a dense fog; all reality is a filmy blur. Perhaps while battling zombies, I had myself become infected. I am tired, thinking about going to work and having to catch up after a week off. More so, I am thinking about being stuck on Hell difficulty. I am not satisfied. My mood has changed quickly. It's difficult to appear happy and pleasant. My wife is upset that I'm eager to get to bed instead of spending a bit of time with her. I make the mistake of telling her I've stayed up until two or three every night playing my new game, and when I am unwilling to stay up an extra thirty minutes to talk to her, she makes me pay for the slip-up:

"You stayed up until two playing a game every night; it's only 12:30 now and you can't visit with your wife who's been gone for four days?"

I am tired, but I stay up and visit; all other alternatives probably involve appeasing an irritated woman, and that will take even longer. I am efficient, after all. When I close my eyes an hour later, I can see and hear only endless zombie carnage. I am frustrated, apprehensive. I hastily offer a feeble prayer to God to help me to go to sleep, but it feels irresponsible to be praying such a prayer in light of the fact that I have put over seventy hours into the game in five days and not prayed a single time during the same time period. As such, I retract the prayer, focus on my breathing, and try to clear my mind. I sleep restlessly, thinking about being stuck in Hell.

Day seven: it seems my vacation vanished in a blink. Sometimes it feels like my whole life is passing in a blink. Most days it's hard to discern whether this is the part of the blink where my eyes are open or the part where my eyes are closed; it all passes in such an indistinct and dizzying haze.

I am tired, irritated, and distracted at work, anxiously browsing online forums, hoping to find answers to the deep mysteries. A mountain of work has piled up in my absence. I consider venting my anger at my wife for keeping me up, but think better of it and manage instead toward maximizing my time in the game. Once home, I tell her Jake kept me up (he crawls into our bed sometimes). He is the scapegoat; he can take one for the team. I'll owe him one. I offer to give the boys a bath and put them to bed if she will let me take a nap, and she takes the bait. After a short catnap, another five hours in the game only furthers my frustration. I feel guilty that I let myself be this affected by a stupid game.

Day eight: I find in an online forum that someone has discovered a glitch[9] that allows them to make more game gold per hour than normal. I am excited to abuse it as soon as possible. For a few hours that night, I exploit the glitch, repeating the same one-minute task several hundred times. I feel a little better about the game. Sure, it has become grossly redundant. Sure, I'm probably in violation of some "user agreement" somewhere that I didn't actually get around to reading before agreeing to it. Yet, even so, it feels there is purpose in it: the clear objective of making steady progress and getting ahead as efficiently as possible. Best not to push it, better quit while I'm ahead; I decide to turn in a little early.

Day nine: in the morning, I check the forums. Players are in a unanimous uproar; the game developers have decided the game is too easy, and they have made a number of specific changes to make it more difficult. If people can beat it in a week, they'll move onto the next game. The developers want their cut of items purchased with real money, and they want to retain as many players as possible for as long as possible.

---

9 An" exploit "technically—using something in the game in a way it was not intended to get ahead or to make more gold per hour than would normally be possible.

In recent years, players have begun to talk about a game's "endgame." After you have exhausted the main content, there has to be something—necessarily somewhat repetitive, since obviously game content is limited—that keeps you playing. Players seek a meaningful and lasting experience. In the past few years this has become exponentially more true than ever before. Hardcore players have become much more selective in the games they play, and they now approach games with the expectation of long-term play. The last game that caught my interest I played for fifteen months, perhaps 1,800 hours, often playing two instances on two different computers at once.[10] I am a serious player looking for serious long-term games; I'm no longer interested in single-player games with twenty-hour plots. I want to be rewarded on a long-term basis; I want lasting meaning. The endgame in *Diablo* is running through the same randomized dungeons over and over in search of randomized loot and gold, always looking forward to finding or buying the next piece of gear that's going to get you a bit closer to besting *Diablo* on Inferno difficulty.

To make the game harder, the developers' solution was to weaken the effectiveness of certain attack skills. Various magic spells and such have been "nerfed" (think nerf football compared to a standard football) to make them less powerful than before. The game that was proving nearly impossible is now impossible for sure. The forums are ablaze with players upset about their characters having just become instantly wimpier. My frustration is mass frustration.

I have fashioned my entire strategy around one skill in particular, and while I was wasting time sleeping, the fates took that mighty skill and contorted it into an emasculated shadow of its former self. I know exactly what the change means for me—my valiant hero is now an incompetent bumbler. My whole strategy disappears in an instant;

---

10 Some role-playing games can be quite redundant ,and each action can take some time to complete ,so many players play the same game twice—two computers ,two monitors ,two controllers at once—to maximize productivity.

countless hours of planning down the pooper. My impotent clown of a character is going to miss out on all of the glory and fortune to be had. I will have to rethink my whole approach. I will practically have to re-learn how to play the game. Enfeebled muddler! I will be the least among my peers! As if to give me one final poke in the eye, they have also fixed my glitch.

Though games are supposed to be fun, I find myself in a world of frustration. I didn't expect this. I didn't see it coming. I thought this would be the one, the game to end all games, the one that satisfies not just for a week or a month but for many years to come. I thought it might even be the promised one I had been waiting for—the one that would satisfy for a lifetime. That optimism is gone now though. I am upset at the game, but even more upset that I let myself be this affected by it.

I need to get away from my desk. Fresh air would be ideal, but heading outside isn't really an option at work. Stagnant, smelly air is, sadly, my next-best option. I head to the public restroom and plant myself on the toilet in the nearest stall. Maybe I should think about taking a break from *Diablo*. Maybe I can think of some other game to tide me over until the release of the next big thing. I lean forward in the stall and rest my face in my hands. I feel overwhelmed and ridiculous, panicked and absurd. My ears begin to ring with loud, indistinct voices. A warm white light slowly grows inside my skull. There is a looming shadow and a fearful apprehension.

4

JUDGMENT BEFORE THE TIME

You always start off thinking each game is so good you'll probably want to play it forever on into eternity, but the optimism always eventually fades, and there is always a little emptiness when it does. The more time and energy you've invested, the greater the emptiness you're left with in the end. The more you've anticipated great emotional heights, the farther your fall back to *terra firma*. This isn't new territory for me—not exactly anyway. It is, no doubt, exacerbated by lack of sleep and putting so many hours in during my week-long bender, but still this feeling is familiar. It's like having finished opening all of the Christmas presents as a kid only to be left thinking, *That's it? What do I do now? What do I look forward to now?* multiplied by a thousand or so. There is always a little guilt. There is always a little conviction. There is always the pursuit of satisfaction, while never quite arriving at satisfaction, like a striving after the wind (Eccl 1.14).

I should have planned for this contingency. In the bathroom, sitting on the can, I hastily begin to rehearse in my mind what life will be like after *Diablo* and what course my life will take from this unexpected turn. My focus centers upon the four- or five-hour span of time at the end of each day that I have carefully honed out for my great love of gaming. I guard this block of time earnestly. I defend it from all enemies, both foreign and domestic. My wife knows I get irritated if the kids are not in bed on time. She knows I begin to stink-eye her any time they stay up too late and it begins to cut into my coveted time. She knows not to invite guests over too late and to keep requests to spend time with me to a minimum in the evenings. This time is the first thing I think about when I get out of bed in the morning and the last thing I think about when falling asleep. This is what keeps me going, what sustains me, what I delight in above all else. My joy is contingent on video games. After about 8:30 p.m., everyone and everything becomes unwelcome background noise.

To my dismay, however, I struggle to conjure an image of what this evening might look like. My mind darts through a long list of potential games, to no avail. There is a whole universe of choices. I own practically every gaming machine on the market. I have four computers, an android device, the latest PlayStation, the latest Xbox, and the latest Nintendo. I also have a top secret pool of money in an undisclosed location, of unspecified amount, reserved for the express purpose of gaming. As far as games go, none are beyond my reach. It is certainly not for lack of opportunity that I can't think of a game worth playing. Nor can it be for lack of awareness that I struggle to think of something to occupy my evenings. I keep a constant eye out for upcoming games. I know every major release scheduled for the next nine months at least. I am practically a scholar of the latest and greatest games, yet still I draw a blank.

As I try to picture how I will occupy my sacred block of time for the next few days and beyond, my imagination seems to go on strike. In the world of games, what has been is what will be; what has been done is what will be done; there is nothing new under the sun. I have had my fill of single-player games where the enemies all behave in cyclical, predictable patterns. I am tired of endlessly frustrating and laggy console shooters and of the entire universe of games without real money in them. I want something different, something new, something more, but I know there's nothing out there. I know there are no prospects for me; I see life without form and void. I see evenings filled with reruns of *Full House* and *The Fresh Prince of Bel-air*, and of going to bed at 8:30 with the boys for lack of content to fill my evenings. I was really banking on *Diablo*.

There are no others that I can hope will sustain me for months to come, and it seems somehow beneath me to begin a game without at least some hope of long-term play. Every hobbyist makes arbitrary distinctions about what is meaningful and what is just "wasting time." To me, anything less than long-term play would just be wasting time.

My future is empty. My happiness is gone. As I try to construct a vision of my immediate future and find myself faltering to do so, the emotion that presses in on me is–unmistakably–hopelessness. It comes upon me powerfully and unexpectedly. It rests deep within my soul, and convinces me its residence is permanent. There will be no reason to get out of bed in the morning. I begin to ask myself the hasty question, "*What will I do now?*" as if I have lost my faith and am now forced to redefine the meaning of it all.

I become increasingly agitated with myself that I could let games have such an effect on me. *Hopeless*? How could a grown man let himself be this affected by a mere game? I'm a business professional, a church-going family man, a grown adult who does all that he pleases. So why do I feel like a slave? Sometimes it feels like no matter how much you feed it, it still wants more. It never seems satisfied, and I'm not sure I'm ever satisfied either.

My ears are ringing. A warm light is growing behind my eyes. I wasn't always this way. I have had seasons of spiritual fervor. There is some vague recollection of what it was like being more zealous for the Gospel than for games. I hear an indistinct murmuring in the back of my brain. I begin to contrast the seriousness of my feelings of loss with the trivial subject matter, and a deep sense of conviction rests upon me. I feel *hopeless* because of *games*. Because of games, I feel hopeless. I went wrong somewhere—a misstep, a missed cue, a wrong turn. I've made something out of nothing, a mountain out of a molehill, as the saying goes. I am *hopeless*, because of *games*. I stand midway between laughing at myself and weeping over myself. For the first time in a long time, I begin to see things for what they really are. A light flickers on in my mind, and thoughts of the game collapse into the shadows, just as my sin grows like a mountain before me. I gaze fearfully upon the monstrosity I have made of things. *Is this even life at all?* The weight of my sin becomes an intolerable burden, as if God has pulled the thin veil away from my double life and is shining a bright light inside, from which I am not permitted to turn away. The lie is exposed. The mask is pulled away. A pattern of sin and addiction is made clear. It feels like The Great Judgment, but before the time (cf. 1 Cor 4.5, Rev 20.11-15).

The voices become more distinct—the words of wise men and texts of scripture I have memorized and read here and there in years gone by. They begin to wound my conscience and to hold me accountable to the truth within me. I have not been honest with myself. Even a cursory glance at my life will tell you my primary motivation for existing is to *play* as much as possible. It won't take a court of divine justice that has access to my inner thoughts to discover this—just look at how I spend my hours, and you will know what is in my heart! Just count up the hours of my day dedicated to this or that, and you will discover my priorities. Listen to what I want to talk about, and you will know what I love above all else. Behold the absurdity; I have sought to find my purpose in games! Like a lifeless zombie traveling mindlessly down the wide road, I have looked to games to give me meaning. I have placed all of my joy in them, though they cannot satisfy me. I have looked to the darkness to fulfill my deepest emotional longings. Like an addict, I sought satisfaction in the wrong place and was left confounded and enslaved. I wasn't always this way though. I vaguely recall the words of Augustine, which left some indelible mark on me in some bygone era:

> *I deserted you, my God. In my youth I wandered away, too far from your sustaining hand, and created of myself a barren waste.*[11]

---

11 Augustine, *Great Books of the Western World*, vol. 18, *The Confessions* (Chicago: Encyclopedia Britannica, 1993), 16.

The real problem isn't *Diablo*. The real problem isn't video games at all. The real problem is something inside, something internal, a darkened understanding, a misdirection of the heart, a broken spiritual compass. I am the kind of person who sees meaning where there is no meaning, who searches the void for satisfaction and significance. I have pursued video games with all of my heart, soul, and mind. There are two, and only two, evils in the world, and I am guilty of both:

> *My people have exchanged their glory*
> *for what has no value.*
> *Be stunned at such a thing, you heavens;*
> *shudder and quake,*
> *declares the Lord.*
> *My people have committed two crimes:*
> *They have forsaken me, the spring of living water.*
> *And they have dug wells, broken wells that can't hold water.*
> *(Jer 2.11b-13 CEB)*

I have worshiped the world. Nothing could be more evident. I am an addict, yes, but that is putting it too politely, for I am an idolater, and addicted to idolatry. I have traded something for nothing, the spring of living waters for a waterless well. I turned from God to pursue a lie of my own devising. I have sought after worthlessness and become worthless (Jer 2.5). By my actions I have shown that I counted the joy of knowing Jesus as worthless in comparison with gaining another level or beating another game. I have traded my glory for what has no value. I have worshiped at a foreign altar and have become as blind and as deaf as my idol (Ps 115.5-8).

I fought the zombie and became the zombie. The words of the apostle Paul, in condemning unbelief, could just as suitably be applied to me:

> *For although they knew God, they did not honor him as God*
> *or give thanks to him, but they became futile in their thinking,*
> *and their foolish hearts were darkened. Claiming to be wise,*

> *they became fools, and exchanged the glory of the immortal God for images...They exchanged the truth about God for a lie and worshiped and served the creature rather than the Creator... (Rom 1.21-25)*

I find myself instantly discontent with what my life has become. In the grand scheme of eternity, life is just a breath (Ps 144.4); I am going to die in just a moment, and my life will have been wasted pursuing a lie—and not even a good one! This is an idol of the most trifling kind, the sort that everyone else chuckles at! I am soon to meet my maker, and when he asks what I have to show for my life, will I tell him my high scores? My trophies? My achievements? My level?

> *I probed the hidden depths of my soul and wrung its pitiful secrets from it, and when I mustered them all before the eyes of my heart, a great storm broke within me, bringing with it a great deluge of tears.*[12]

I am wounded, ashamed, crying quietly in the public restroom and praying haphazardly. The future is uncertain.

---

12 Augustine, *Great Books of the Western World*, vol. 18, *The Confessions* (Chicago: Encyclopedia Britannica, 1993), 76.

5

DEVELOPING PATTERNS

Where did I go wrong? When did I stray from the narrow path? Let me take a moment to retrace the steps that brought me to this point. I turned thirty-three this year; I suppose I'm among the oldest of those who cannot remember a time before video games. As I was in my youth, so too were video games, and in some ways, it almost feels like we've matured together. As a child with an Atari, I could be an airplane pilot, a medieval warrior, a tank commander, or a pong master. The sky was the limit really, and a little practice reaped many rewards. Back then you couldn't "save" your progress; you just started from scratch, back at the very beginning each time. There wasn't much by way of simulated physics; it was mostly just a 1:1 correlation between the joystick and the movement of a small congregation of pixels on the screen, but it seemed to me a glorious sort of magic. The emotional reward was usually just beating my brother's high score, but that was plenty—more than enough really. It was ground-breaking technology—an 8-bit processor which could run up to 1.1 megahertz, with 128 colors. It was $199 at release in 1976. We had one TV in the house and could sneak an hour in after school before Dad got home from work and wanted to watch the news. The rest of the night and next day would be spent strategizing for our one hour the next day; we would be ready.

The original Nintendo Entertainment System stole Atari's role as the dominant home game console in the mid-1980s, but I never owned one. My mom refused it, enduring countless hours of nagging. Maybe she had taken note of a not-so-subtle preoccupation with gaming, or—more likely—maybe she had just grown tired of fighting for the TV. I sought out friendships with more fortunate souls who had been blessed with both a Nintendo and parents who allowed frequent sleepovers, and I would play to the point of exhaustion on every such occasion. There were a couple of obnoxious and smelly kids I didn't even really care for, but it was important to stay in their good graces nonetheless; it seemed a fair social contract.

The Sega Genesis made its way into our house. I remember *Sonic the Hedgehog*, *Shining Force*, *Streets of Rage* and *Mortal Kombat*. Competition was always invigorating in games like *Mortal Kombat*, and knocking my older brother's virtual head off after beating him in a match was exceptionally satisfying; we were more than willing to leave the ethical questions to someone else. The only commandments that concerned us much at the time were "Finish him!" and "Get over here!" Role-playing games like *Shining Force* and *Shining in the Darkness* seemed to offer more benefits to long-term play. Now you would start as a peasant and, with dedication, end up a kingly demigod. The concept of leveling a character, of growing progressively stronger as you played through the game, proved to be a powerful and persuasive motivational force. It eventually made its way into pretty much every game on the market and made points and high scores seem like childish rewards by comparison.

The early days of the original Sony PlayStation offered more of the same, but virtual worlds were now rendered in polygons in three dimensions. Despite the busyness of high school and the first couple years of college, I spent countless hours over at friends' houses playing games like *Tekken 2* and *Twisted Metal 2*. The system brought innovations with titles like *Gran Turismo*, a racing simulator. Instead of squealing around turns at 200 mph, now you had to brake before turning, steer into the apex of the turn, and accelerate out of the corner. You had to think through racing physics and try to maximize the grip of each tire. You had to plan ahead and position yourself to enter and exit each turn correctly. You even had to take virtual driving classes inside the game. Realistic physics made it impossible to master, extending the lifespan of the game considerably.

Then there was *Grand Theft Auto 3*. The concept of pulling some unfortunate driver out of his car, jumping in, and driving away with his ride was inherently fun, but coupled with running him over with said ride after you had stolen it made GTA3 an instant hit with every gamer I knew.[13] Probably more significantly, it was a "sandbox" game. No longer did you go through a linear plot. Here you were in a wide open world and could do whatever you pleased. If you wanted to drive around and commit random crimes—robbing stores, stealing cars, mugging pedestrians, beating up hookers, collecting fares for driving a taxi cab, whatever—you could get rewarded with cash to buy weapons and cars. There were multiple storylines at once, and players could follow whichever path they wanted. There was no set way to accomplish any given mission. You could go in the front door with a bazooka like Rambo or sneak around back with a silenced pistol, assassin style. Either way, the havoc was gratifying, and the scale of the destruction was epic. The concept of clearing a level through redundant play and memorizing where to jump and duck, like in the days of Mario and Sonic, again seemed shallow by comparison. Through college, living away from home without any real restrictions upon playing time, I probably played around four or five hours most days, while going to class (most of the time) and working part time.

I bought a PlayStation 2 coming out of college and going into graduate school. I played every major release, each introducing minor improvements over the last. Many games could now hold a player's

13 I will speak of video game content more later. For the present, I am only speaking of my feelings at the time and not making implicit claims of this or that being morally acceptable or not.

attention for 100 hours or more. I worked thirty hours a week while going to school part time. I studied Christian Theology and the history of philosophy on my own for several hours most days, but as a single bachelor (without any prospects!) in my mid-twenties, I still found four hours or so to play each day. I lived with my parents again, and still there was only one television, so I would wake up at noon, work in the afternoon (or go to school in the afternoon on school days) come home and read until midnight or so, and after my parents were in bed I would play until around 4:00 a.m. Often I would awkwardly pass my dad in the hallway as I was heading to bed and he was getting up for work. I liked my schedule; there seemed to be time enough for God and games, and there was a clearly designated time for each. Often I would skip the gaming altogether and read late into the night. It was a spiritual high water mark for me. I fought against sin persistently during these few years, I sought to understand the God of the Bible to the best of my ability, and in many ways, video games took an appropriate back seat.

Yet I had, by this time, deferred adulthood as long as I was able and could no longer outpace it. It swept over me like a great tsunami. In the span of five years, I had a "real job," was married, and had two boys. Those big life changes seemed to happen very quickly. For several years, I felt a great deal of discontent about how little I was able to play. I worked from 8:00 to 5:00, and the kids went to bed at 8:30, subject to daily random variations. My job was very technical and learning-intensive, so I had to go to bed by 11:00 to get a good night's sleep, so as not to feel overwhelmed each day. It's the common lot of all parents with young kids to always feel strapped for time. Gaming was often a point of contention between my wife and me. Understandably, I was not satisfying her need to spend *some* "alone time" with me, and she wasn't satisfying my need to play games for a stated minimum of three or four hours per day (which would have simply been impossible). When I lived with my parents and had minimal responsibilities, I could have God and games both, but after we had kids it felt like either God or games had to go if I was to pursue the other to my satisfaction. Not dramatically or all at once, of course, but gradually over time, I made a clear choice. I wish I could say I didn't realize it. Certainly my vision was clouded in certain ways, yet I understood the choice I was making to some degree. Mostly, I just did what the world does and tried not to think about it. The old Puritan, Jeremiah Burroughs (c. 1600-1646), knew how it works:

> *A man who has a bad conscience does not care to look into his own soul, but loves to be out, and to look into other things; he never looks to himself.*[14]

We live noisy, fast-paced lives, and we fear silence, because in silence we might have to stop and look inside and examine our ways. It's better just to be out and about and constantly entertained. In my case, this was expedited by the new frontier of online gaming. All of a sudden, I could play a first-person shooter like *Battlefield* or *Medal of Honor* with sixteen or more players online, with live voice chat, all running around trying to kill one another. It was satisfying to hear my opponent grumbling in protest on the other end after I had ended his miserable, virtual existence. Now single-player, offline games in general felt shallow. Here was real, substantial, human competition, up close and personal. The notion of playing against the computer or NPCs (non-player characters) seemed shallow to me by comparison. It was time to stop playing kids' games and get serious.

I also enjoyed online role-playing games. Take a game like *Runescape* or *World of Warcraft*. These are MMORPGs (massive multiplayer online role-playing games). Here players can make friends with real people and adventure and fight in a persistent[15] sandbox world. There is seemingly limitless potential for character growth, and a seemingly

---

14 Jeremiah Burroughs, *The Rare Jewel of Christian Contentment* (1648; repr., Carlisle, PA: The Banner of Truth Trust, 2009), 77.

15 "persistent" in the sense that even when you log out, it is still there.

limitless number of skills and trades to explore. There are a countless number of both short-term and long-term rewards. When you tire of one task or trade, you can seamlessly move on to the next. The lifespan of a game goes from a couple of weeks to months, if not years. These games can be constantly expanded and updated on the fly to ensure that no player ever quits because he reached the end or achieved all there is to achieve. Being higher level than others gives you bragging rights and draws compliments and envy from other players. There is only success behind you and only promises of getting better and being more powerful ahead of you. There is no "beating the game" here, no end to speak of. It is a constant and endless IV drip of "you win." Even gamers are appalled by this statistic: an astronomical 5.93 million years have been invested into playing the game *World of Warcraft*.[16]

Diablo brought many of these elements together. It's an online action game with many role-playing elements. It is social (or not, whichever you please); it is competitive (or not); it offers an innumerable multitude of short- and long-term rewards. It is, in all fairness, a very fun game; many people will play it every day, for many hours each day, for many years to come. There's no question about that. The real icing on the cake though, at least for me, was the element of having real money in the game. When I start making paychecks, I thought, my wife would never again be able to suggest that perhaps I was investing too much energy into video games and how she hadn't seen me reading or trying to write in a while. (How it got under my skin when she exposed my lie by simply stating the obvious!) Now gaming would be a second job, lending it social credibility, offering less self-doubt. No longer would I be just another overweight gamer, apathetic to most of the rest of my life and surroundings, but rather I would now be supporting my family to the best of my ability, taking up the call of duty, and sacrificing myself

16 "If All of Work Were Gamified", BloombergBusinessweek, last modified May 24, 2011, accessed July 28, 2012, http://www.businessweek.com/managing/content/may2011/ca20110524_211203.htm.

on their behalf. As far as addictions go, people respect workaholics way more than they respect video game addicts, so it seemed a commendable upgrade.

I began to see a pattern developing as I would recount this nearly thirty-year history to myself from time to time. Each new generation of games made me feel I had wasted my time with the last generation. How trivial it was playing *Mario Brothers* or *Sonic the Hedgehog* as a kid and figuring out where every single hidden coin and extra life was. Once I had discovered competitive online multiplayer games, how silly, I thought, playing countless single-player games where the enemies telegraph their next intention and are designed to be utterly predictable. Online made offline feel trivial; multiplayer made single-player feel trivial; levelling up your character made high scores feel trivial; earning real money made earning virtual gold feel trivial. The more I played, the more I longed for a deeper experience and the more I found that my desire for depth—for a genuinely satisfying experience—outpaced even the feverish speed of new game releases, each better than the last.

I had also grown familiar with the psychological stages involved in video game addiction. I knew how it moved quickly from simple enjoyment to a sort of fiendish obsession. Early on, when addiction is at its peak, I would be very irritated if I were forced to skip a day playing and would be constantly anxious about not having enough time to play. Eventually, after the newness had begun to wear off and the grind had begun to set in, I would arrive at a more socially acceptable level of addiction, which could be sustained for a few weeks or a few months. Then, finally, frustration, boredom, and mild anxiety would set in as my interest in the game waned, and I began searching for the next big fix in the next big thing. With each new game, there was a predictable and perpetual cycle, always ending ultimately in dissatisfaction.

We turn lots of perfectly good things into idols simply by letting them distract our attention away from God. Without ever so much as a single thought about it, we quietly place them upon the pedestal of our hearts as the primary object of our affection, and thereby give them the highest place in our lives. We can make an addiction out of anything. Yet we were not designed to be satisfied by such things. Listen to Burroughs again:

> *That is just as if a man were hungry, and to satisfy his craving stomach he should gape and hold open his mouth to take in the wind, and then should think that the reason why he is not satisfied is because he has not got enough of the wind; no, the reason is because the thing is not suitable to a craving stomach. Yet there is really the same madness in the world: the wind which a man takes in by gaping will as soon satisfy a craving stomach ready to starve, as all the comforts in the world can satisfy a soul who knows what true happiness means.* [17]

In the moment of conviction in the bathroom, the words of the psalmist were ringing in my ears:

> *To all perfection I see a limit, but your commands are boundless. (Ps 119.96 NIV)*

There is a limit to the perfection of every earthly thing. The best of songs grows old with time. Too much of the best of foods makes the taste of it obnoxious. Too much fuss over games sucks all the fun right out of it. It is madness to rest our hope and joy on such things. The God of Heaven and Earth, on the other hand, does not admit of such limitations. He is both able and willing to satisfy man's every desire indefinitely:

> *The law of the Lord is perfect,*
> *reviving the soul;*
> *the testimony of the Lord is sure,*
> *making wise the simple;*

---

17 Jeremiah Burroughs, *The Rare Jewel of Christian Contentment* (1648; repr., Carlisle, PA: The Banner of Truth Trust, 2009), 91.

the precepts of the Lord are right,
rejoicing the heart;
the commandment of the Lord is pure,
enlightening the eyes;
the fear of the Lord is clean,
enduring forever;
the rules of the Lord are true,
and righteous altogether.
More to be desired are they than gold,
even much fine gold;
sweeter also than honey
and drippings of the honeycomb.
Moreover, by them is your servant warned;
in keeping them there is great reward. (Ps 19.7-11)

I had become conscious of these thoughts to some degree, but I chose to continue in my self-deception, and I suppressed them. Like Bruce Banner and the Incredible Hulk, the man wrestled to get out at times, but the monster always overcame him. I pushed the conviction deep down into some dark corner. I had a hundred different lies to keep me going: How could I possibly be spiritually productive with two little kids hanging on me all day? I couldn't very well come home and read my Bible all night or try to study or write after a long day of work; a night of leisure was my due. Everyone has something; it's not as if video games are unethical or illegal. I could be doing much worse; I go to church on Sundays, and I pay my mortgage on time.

I'm still doing better than most people, I reasoned. I'm still a productive member of society. I'm no different from the sports fan who knows the names and statistics of each player, who theorizes about possible outcomes based on a complex set of data, who enjoys the learning curve given the complexity of the subject matter, who offers his time, money, and energy to his primary passion in life, even though, in the end, it all seems to add up to nothing. It could be stamp collecting; it could be bicycling; it could be a job; it could be any hobby, profession, habit, actor, author, singer, anyone. It could—literally—be anything at all. Everyone is addicted to something, I told myself, and mine is gaming.

I could even twist the Bible to my bidding. I often rehearsed this one to myself: "The unmarried man is anxious about the things of the Lord, how to please the Lord. But the married man is anxious about worldly things, how to please his wife, and his interests are divided" (I Cor 7.32b-34). The Apostle was giving me a wink that it was okay and to be expected. Married men are supposed to be distracted from thoughts about God—that's just how it goes. I was practically fulfilling prophecy!

There were a host of other lies. Every accusation of conscience would be quickly struck down with a handy assortment of excuses (cf. Rom 2.15). Another Puritan, Thomas Watson (1620-1686), noted that "there is no sin that does not labor either to hide itself under some mask or, if it cannot be concealed, then to vindicate itself by some apology."[18] If all else failed, I could always appease my conscience by telling myself that sometime in the future, when the boys were older, I would straighten myself up a bit and try to be a better example of godliness. As is the common lot of man, I wanted to be a better person, just not quite yet. The great philosopher and theologian, Saint Augustine (AD 354-430), the bishop of Hippo (what is now Algeria, Africa), struggled with the sin of lust:

> *I had prayed to you for chastity and said, "give me chastity and continence, but not yet." for I was afraid that you would answer my prayer at once and cure me too soon of the disease of lust which I wanted satisfied, not quelled.*[19]

---

18 Thomas Watson, *The Art of Divine Contentment* (Grand Rapids, MI: Soli Deo Gloria Publications, 2011), 31.

19 Augustine of Hippo, *Great Books of the Western World*, vol. 18, *The Confessions* (Chicago: Encyclopedia Britannica, 1993), 72.

While my repertoire of lies was substantial and even on Sunday mornings I could put up a respectable facade, I was a spiritual dead man, a lifeless zombie, a hollow Christian shell. The name of Jesus sounded to me more like an acquaintance I used to know than a Master, Savior, and Brother to whom I owed a debt of eternal gratitude. I didn't read my Bible, let alone other books. I couldn't pray without feeling guilty about it. Even the best of Sunday morning sermons would fall on deaf ears. My happiness would come and go like the ocean tide. Too many times I snapped at my wife over being frustrated with a game, but was too embarrassed to admit as much. Instead, I would just let her believe her first inclination—that she had done something wrong. My life was an embarrassment; how could I even look my little boys in the eyes any longer? I was getting so tired of rushing through an obligatory playtime with them, thinking all the while about getting back upstairs and leaving them again under the watchful care of the Disney Channel. I was growing weary of chasing after more "realistic" games while, at the same time, letting reality pass me by.

> *I felt that I was still the captive of my sins, and in my misery I kept crying "How long shall I go on saying 'tomorrow, tomorrow'? Why not now? Why not make an end of my ugly sins at this moment?"*[20]

In the bathroom, it was obvious to me that God was dealing with me, disciplining me as a loving Father (cf. Heb 12.6). He had flicked on a spiritual light somewhere inside of me, awakened me from my spiritual slumber, made me discontent with my life of sinful addiction and of world worship, and was going to show me a better path. What was unthinkable yesterday was today a reality. I decided, at the very least, I needed to reset my priorities, to reckon with my God and my idols, to take a serious and sober break from video games—the first of its kind in my thirty-three years.

---

20 Ibid.76 ,

6

BLESSED MISERY

The first night, it feels as if *Diablo* himself, down there on Inferno difficulty, is calling me to battle, taunting me, laughing at my folly for crying like a school girl in a public john. There are more places to see, more things to do, more zombies needing to be taught a lesson. There is still time enough to change my mind and to shake off the conviction. I can just chalk it up to odd sleep habits and press on toward the prize of virtual glory.

I can hardly believe I'm not going to play the game I waited a year for and dropped sixty bucks on just a few days ago. I always tell myself the more mileage I get out of a game, the better steward I've been of my money, and here I am being wasteful. If I play a $60 game for 10 hours, then I've paid $6.00 per hour. If, on the other hand, I play the same game 2000 hours, then I've only spent three cents an hour.[21] Plus I have spent a week stockpiling gold to sell on the soon-to-be-released real money auction house. That's a double waste. There's no telling how much cash I'll miss out on. I could be missing out on a mountain of real money, for all I know.[22]

---

21 I suppose this implies the value of my time is, at best, -$.03/per hour. The curious thing about gaining the world and losing your soul (Mt 16.26) is that you actually lose both over the long term.

22 I checked some months later, and I believe my 70 hours of labor was worth about $12.00. The real money auction house was eventually discontinued

Yet the weight of my sin is far too heavy to ignore. Am I even a Christian? If I believe in the God of the Bible—really believe!—can I justify the course my life has taken over the past couple of years? Would I be living the way I am if I believe life is a fog that appears in the morning and then quickly vanishes (Jas 4.14) and that I am, therefore, terminally ill, waiting for imminent death? Do I believe that, if I love the world, the love of the Father is not in me (1 Jn 2.15)? That there are eternal rewards to be gained for spiritual success (Mt 5.12)? That there is a spiritual battle going on in the universe (Eph 6.12)? That men's lives hang in the balance? That Jesus himself is pleading with his Father for me—this very instant!—to be gracious to me despite clear shortcomings (Rom 8.34)? That if I love him, I will keep his commandments (Jn 14.15)? That he knows all (Ps 147.5)? That there is soon to be a Great Judgment in which everything done in secret will be brought to light (Lk 8.17)? If I believe even one of these, among countless others of equal weight, would I be treating God as some peripheral part of my life? Would I continue pretending he isn't right here with me always, taking exhaustive notes on all of my actions and whereabouts? Would I be paying him his due between 9:00 and 11:00 on Sunday morning and then getting back to the real (virtual) stuff of life?

I'm not exactly sure what to do with myself after the boys are in bed. There is a four-hour span of time that has been completely booked up for years, and now it is completely empty. Whereas finding enough time was a stressful burden yesterday, today the burden is having too much. The night seems endless, the way prison inmates describe "the hole" of solitary confinement. I'm doing all the right things I suppose: I read a little, write a little, listen to a sermon about happiness, pray for comfort and forgiveness, go to bed an hour early, yet I wake up feeling even worse than before.

The morning brings withdrawal symptoms of a spiritual sort. The cravings come in the form of a question: *Is this it?* Is this the Christian

---

because the developers decided that it ruined the core gameplay.

life? Is this what it's all about? Am I to trade the life of video game thrills for the monastic life of reading dusty old books and listening to the droning of monotone sermons? After a long day of reading boring, technical books at work, will I forgo the excitement of bludgeoning zombies to a gruesome pulp in exchange for a sleepy night of reading through the genealogies of the book of Numbers or the tabernacle dimensions in Exodus? Virtual reality can look pretty good when measured against the backdrop of a bleak reality.

I'm asking the Author of the Universe how he can compete with organized pixels, and how his ancient words can stack up against the latest and greatest moving pictures, and I'm a bit ashamed about it, of course, but there's no denying that's the question I'm confronted with. Sure, the satisfaction of video games is short lived—trivial at best—and sure, the Bible holds out eternal rewards unspeakable. But let's face it, when we get right down to it, every overweight American attests to the fact that human beings will almost never—if ever—defer immediate pleasure for long-term gain. Given the choice between this piece of pie or a trim future waistline and a longer life, our choice is most evident. We carry the evidence around with us wherever we go. There is, as it were, a glut of evidence against us.

Similarly, given the choice between a short and instantly gratifying sitcom or a chapter out of a good book, which will sharpen our mind into something better, we choose the TV 99% of the time, and the other 1% of the time we choose wisely only because we feel guilty about the 99% wasted. We would all hold ten doctorate degrees and be world-class triathletes if this were not so. It's in everything we do. The promise of indistinct future treasures in heaven offers little incentive to the chronically bored, media-saturated, 21st century American. Let's be honest. Sin is easy and immediately satisfying; self-control and perseverance sound sleepy in their very conception. Sin is a roller coaster with no waiting in line, and the quiet life of devotion seems a lot like a slow and somber walk with Grandma at "the home."

I wrestle with this for weeks, unsettled by such irreligious thoughts in the midst of my turning away from addiction, yet still more unsettled by the prospect of wasting my life being apathetically entertained. I think to myself that I just need to work up enough determination to figure out a way to suffer through the boring Christian life and to forgo the great pleasures of sin for another fifty years or so, in order that I might gain the endless life of singing boring hymns forever.

Though none of my prospects strike me as particularly satisfying, still I feel like God has begun something in me. I feel as if he is unwilling for me to turn back, that he will drag me or carry me if need be. The words of Augustine resonate with my own experience:

> *What crooked paths I trod! What dangers threatened my soul when it rashly hoped that by abandoning you it would find something better! Whichever way it turned, on front or back or sides, it lay on a bed that was hard, for in you alone the soul can rest. You are there to free from the misery of error which leads us astray, to set us on your own path and to comfort us by saying, "Run on, for I shall hold you up. I shall lead you and carry you on to the end."*[23]

I hold on tightly to the words of James, who knew what leading a double life was all about:

> *Submit yourselves therefore to God. Resist the devil, and he will flee from you. Draw near to God, and he will draw near to you. Cleanse your hands, you sinners, and purify your hearts, you double-minded. Be wretched and mourn and weep. Let your laughter be turned to mourning and your joy to gloom. Humble yourselves before the Lord, and he will exalt you. (Jas 4.7-10)*

---

23 Augustine of Hippo, *Great Books of the Western World*, vol. 18, *The Confessions* (Chicago: Encyclopedia Britannica, 1993), 54.

I am miserable, for sure, but according to James, misery seems to be the order of the day. Here is a promise I can cling to and do cling to; there is hope for me. If I continue drawing near to God humbly, with nothing at all to offer him and in need of much grace in return, he will be true to his promise as well and draw closer to me. I cling to the great biblical truth that the promises of God are certain; he will not lie or change his mind about his promises:

God is not man, that he should lie,
or a son of man, that he should change his mind.
Has he said, and will he not do it?
Or has he spoken, and will he not fulfill it? (Num 23.19)

Make no mistake, things are easy when you swim with the tide, and difficult when you decide to war against it. But such is "repentance," literally "to change one's mind." Repentance is deciding to swim against the tide of the world and of our own sin, in light of the fact that our natural inclination is to swim with it. As Christians, we often think of repentance as a one-time event we experience when we first come to believe, and while saving faith certainly comes with repentance, it's also important to keep in mind that godly repentance characterizes the whole Christian experience. We meet every stage of our Christian growth with mourning over the prior era of sin, as we stand now from a higher vantage point, being a little less worldly and a little more spiritual, a little less earth and a little more heaven.[24]

---

24 The initial repentance from sin and forgiveness of sin in Christ is commonly called "justification." The Christian is once and for all free of the guilt of sin, since Jesus' blood has "atoned" for, or "covered over" their sins. Then the ongoing process of repentance is commonly called "sanctification" as God's children always strive to be more like their great hero, Jesus, and their Father in heaven. A key thing to remember about justification and sanctification is that you can't have one without the other. A person has both or neither, but never just one or the other.

I ask forgiveness for my sins and I repent. I turn away from video game addiction. I become determined, by God's grace, to systematically review and change every last one of my habits until my life is centered upon God once again. My conscience is clean for the first time in a few years. Although my vision is far from clear, I know for certain the way back is a lie and the way forward is backed by a multitude of promises which are sure. I know that the frustration, sorrow, and upset stemming from gaming is worthless, leading nowhere, but sorrow for one's sin is a life raft leading to a life with no regrets:

> *For godly grief produces a repentance that leads to salvation without regret, whereas worldly grief produces death. For see what earnestness this godly grief has produced in you, but also what eagerness to clear yourselves, what indignation, what fear, what longing, what zeal, what punishment! At every point you have proved yourselves innocent in the matter. (2 Cor 7.10-11)*

I am miserable, yes, but there is a worse misery. Not always theologically sound, the (arguably) Christian philosopher Søren Kierkegaard (1813-1855), nevertheless has moments of clarity. True "despair," for Kierkegaard, is failing to define yourself in terms of the infinite God. "Despair" in this sense is not subjective, from our point of view, but objective, from God's point of view. Just as a sick man is sick even if he chooses to deny it, so too the unbeliever is in "despair" even if he thinks he is fine. The Christian despairs of sin and dies to sin to gain life, but the unbeliever lives for sin, is in despair, and gains only death:

> *...that man's life is wasted who lived on, so deceived by the joys of life or by its sorrows that he never became eternally and decisively conscious of himself as spirit, as self, or (what is the same thing) never became aware and in the deepest sense received an impression of the fact that there is a God, and that he, he himself, his self, exists before this God, which gain of infinity*

> *is never attained except through despair. And, oh, this misery, that so many live on and are defrauded of this most blessed of all thoughts; this misery, that people employ themselves about everything else...[when] they might gain the highest thing, the only thing worth living for, and enough to live in for an eternity—it seems to me that I could weep for an eternity over the fact that such misery exists!...And, oh, when the hour-glass has run out, the hourglass of time, when the noise of worldliness is silenced, and the restless [and] ineffectual busyness comes to an end...whether thou wast man or woman, rich or poor, dependent or independent, fortunate or unfortunate, whether thou didst bear the splendor of the crown in a lofty station, or didst bear only the labor and heat of the day in an inconspicuous lot; whether thy name shall be remembered as long as the world stands (and so was remembered as long as the world stood), or without a name thou didst cohere as nameless with the countless multitude... eternity asks of thee and of every individual among these million millions only one question, whether thou has lived in despair or not...and if so, if thou has lived in despair...then for thee all is lost, eternity knows thee not, it never knew thee...*[25]

I pray frequently for help and clear direction. Despite the impression I have left so far, like a proper American male I never cry, but on the way to and from work nearly every day for weeks, crying seems to become a regular part of my daily routine. Surely God has some other purpose for me! Surely I can be of some use still! Surely my life is not intended to be wasted completely. Surely this sorrow is the work of the Holy Spirit in me and not just male PMS or something.

---

25 Søren Kierkegaard, *The Sickness Unto Death* (Princeton, NJ: Princeton University Press, 1941), 26-27. It should be noted that Kierkegaard wrote this work under a pseudonym and never claimed that his own views aligned with any or all of his various aliases.

I pray not to return to my former ways. I walk fearfully—fearful of this repentance lasting only a day or two and reverting to things as they were. On the way to and from work, I avoid my regular "shock jock" radio talk shows; I can't imagine they have been helping anything either. I trade them in for the Bible on CD, the book of Proverbs mostly. I keep my ears peeled for something uplifting, since I more or less detest being around myself.

I am fearful of replacing one vice for another. I try to avoid overeating—another proclivity of mine—and I make it a point to not just replace video games with TV or some other form of entertainment. By and large I avoid all entertainment media. I just feel too weak to deal with any of it right now. Plus, like a true gamer, I have always felt that the passive entertainment of watching TV is lousy entertainment anyway, so no sense trading entertainment I really like just for entertainment I like less, when both seem equally fruitless.

I also have to resist the temptation over the next few weeks to simply fall into depression and sleep my life away. The heart is desperately wicked. Even depression and emotional darkness can be an idol on which we focus our attention, in which we take some strange prideful satisfaction. There are steep cliffs on every side of us in this world. There are as many potential addictions as there are *things* in the world. It is surely true that the road to destruction is wide and easy and the road to life is hard and narrow (Mt 7.13-14).

Unhappy with all of the prospects before me, I continue with my ill-conceived plan and each day add to the promises of God that I know are dependable. I fast frequently (another first for me); I pray purposefully at scheduled times each day; I read my Bible as if it is a treasure map and I'm getting close to the "X." I listen to the Bible in the car to and from work. I read more each week than I have read in the previous year. I listen to sermons of trustworthy men. I read books by trustworthy men. I avoid all entertainment media; I avoid oversleeping (although I do catch up on some much-needed sleep); I avoid overeating. I carefully consider what I look at, what I listen to, what I think about. Surely such a path cannot end badly? Though the present is dark, I am hopeful that light is ahead, just around the corner, though I cannot now see it. I must learn to walk by faith, and not by sight (2 Cor 5:7).

7

DECEITFUL DESIRES

Now this I say and testify in the Lord, that you must no longer walk as the Gentiles do, in the futility of their minds. They are darkened in their understanding, alienated from the life of God because of the ignorance that is in them, due to their hardness of heart. They have become callous and have given themselves up to sensuality, greedy to practice every kind of impurity. But that is not the way you learned Christ!—assuming that you have heard about him and were taught in him, as the truth is in Jesus, to put off your old self, which belongs to your former manner of life and is corrupt through deceitful desires, and to be renewed in the spirit of your minds, and to put on the new self, created after the likeness of God in true righteousness and holiness. (Eph 4.17-24)

I have lots of time to think about the "deceitful desires" Paul mentions here. Our sinful desires are deceitful because they promise the world, and when it comes time to collect, they always come up empty. Sin always promises the experience of our lifetime, but the end result is wrought with dissatisfaction, since sin leads us away from God. Just like the drug addict, we end up focusing entirely on the ounce of pleasure we get from our sin and we have to try to tune out the fifty pounds of misery that come right alongside. John Piper has it right: "Deceitful desires can trick us into feeling sinful thoughts and acts will be more satisfying than seeing God. This illusion is so strong that it creates moral confusion, so that people find ways to justify sin as good, or, if not good, at least permissible."[26]

Sin's primary goal is to distract us from God by making itself appear attractive and by making righteousness appear unattractive. It does this by secretly deforming our thinking and by convincing us that sin is our better option. Our deceitful desires trick us into thinking that evil is good and good is evil. When Adam and Eve decided to eat of the Tree of Knowledge of Good and Evil, they did so because they believed there was something to be gained from it. The fruit seemed to contain amazing mysteries and endless discovery. It looked good, it smelled good, and the serpent assured them it contained instant wisdom—the same sort of wisdom God had (Gen 3.5-6). Besides, God had pronounced that his entire creation was "very good" (Gen 1.31), including the fruit of this tree. There was every reason to believe this fruit would taste good, just like every other fruit in the garden. It was just a little bite of a little fruit, after all.

It's basically the same for us. Nobody chooses to sin because they think it will bring them less pleasure or happiness than choosing righteousness. We choose sin precisely because we think sin will be more fun and more satisfying than obedience, and that the wages of sin are better than the wages of righteousness. We choose sin because we think there's some benefit to be gained from it. I built my life around video games simply because, at some level, I thought it was my best option. Just as Adam and Eve thought some blessing was hidden in that fruit, so too, I looked to video games to satisfy me simply because that's where I believed satisfaction was most likely to be found.

In truth, we know there was something much more sinister behind

---

26 John Piper, *When I Don't Desire God: How to Fight for Joy* (Wheaton, IL: Crossway Books, 2004), 102.

Adam and Eve's decision. God had planted the tree there so they might prove their fidelity to him, so he could reward them for doing so. God's purpose for it was not to trip them up—that would have been completely out of character; his purpose for it was good. Satan's temptation, however, forced Adam and Eve to decide whether God really had their best interests in mind or whether he was merely trying to keep them in the dark about some wonderful secret he knew. They began to question whether God was good, whether he was dependable, whether there was greater satisfaction to be found in sin than in obedience. In order for sin to win the victory over them, it had to make them doubt whether God was really looking out for them. In the end, they turned away from God and came to trust more in the fruit and their own understanding than in God himself. The fruit itself was insignificant; the real question was what did their sin say about God? Eating the fruit meant they had to first believe God was a liar. They called evil good, and they called good evil. Adam and Eve had been distracted by the world, and their sin tricked them into missing the bigger picture. They learned the painful lesson that sin only pays with death (Rom 6.23), and death is never satisfied (Pr 27.20).

We are all like our father, Adam. Each of us in our turn takes the fruit from the tree, elevates it above God, interprets it without regard to God, and uses it as an end in itself, as a means of finding happiness. We kid ourselves into believing the things God made can make us happier than God himself can make us, that we can be wiser and happier on our own, left to our own devices. Therefore, we cast a skeptical eye on God, and consider him a sort of out-of-touch buzzkill. We see him as a burdensome judge looking over our shoulder to convict us, rather than as a loving Father, checking in because he's concerned for us. We question whether it's our best interest or his best interest that he *really* has in mind. All day long, every day of our lives, we choose between resentment and gratefulness, and, if we're honest, we make the wrong choice all the time.

It starts as a seed—as a subtle lie, probably mixed with a half-truth (like all really believable lies)—but "sin when it is fully grown, brings forth death" (Jas 1.15). At first, I just cut back on a little reading, so I could have a bit more time to play. But over time, little by little, games seemed to grow in importance and began to crowd out everything else. First it was a little reading, then a little Bible reading, then a church event here and there, then Christian fellowship, and then, after a couple of years down the road, I barely even prayed anymore. Sin was winning in me, but I didn't fully see what was happening.

Now all of this is very somber and serious talk for a book that is otherwise filled to the brim with bathroom and toilet euphemisms, but there is a key point to be grasped here if we are to make any progress: sin's primary goal is to distract us from God, and one of its greatest tactics is the use of the smallest of things—things which are good in themselves. Adam and Eve didn't lie; they didn't steal; they didn't murder. They just misused God's good creation. They used what was good in a way that was evil. To gain the victory, Satan wanted Eve to focus not on what her action said about God, how it might affect her relationship with God, or what the long-term effects might be, but more just on the good thing itself and what might be gained from it in the short term. Satan wanted her to focus on the ounce of pleasure to be had right now rather than the fifty pounds of suffering that would follow in the wake. Eve "saw that the tree was good for food, and that it was a delight to the eyes, and that the tree was to be desired to make one wise" (Gen 3.6).[27]

Sin's goal in us is just to keep us focused on what is at hand and distracted from looking at the bigger picture. We don't need to murder; we don't need to steal. Those are, in fact, too obvious for sin's taste—better that we not know we're sinners at all, lest we be discontented with ourselves. Sin only needs to keep us entertained and distracted, focused on the world and not on God, just content enough not to want to rock

27 It's worth noting that sin has no creative abilities of its own. It merely takes God's creation and twists it for some inappropriate purpose.

the boat, just trapped enough not to realize our true predicament, just blind enough not to know we're lost. Like zombies on the wide road, we don't see where we're headed because the darkness has blinded our eyes (1 Jn 2.11). Sin succeeds generally not by throwing us into some horrific and blatant sin, but by subtly convincing us there is more joy to be found in entertainment and hobbies than in prayer and Bible reading. Sin destroys our appetite for spiritual nourishment, thereby enticing us down the pathway of spiritual malnutrition. As the gentle coming and going of the tide eventually carves deep channels into the land, so too does sin slowly erode our desire for God and for righteousness. The demon in C.S. Lewis' *Screwtape Letters* admits as much to his protégé, Wormwood:

> *It does not matter how small the sins are provided that their cumulative effect is to edge the man away from the Light and out into the nothing. Murder is no better than cards if cards can do the trick. Indeed the safest road to Hell is the gradual one—the gentle slope, soft underfoot, without sudden turnings, without milestones, without signposts.*[28]

The murderer might see his blood-soaked hands and come to recognize the darkness in his soul, but the card player will almost certainly never consider it. The point is not that there's something wrong with playing cards or video games or any other "pastime," for that matter; the point is that the sin in you wants you to lead a wasted and ineffective life. It doesn't matter what you waste your life on. The smaller the thing, the better, as far as sin is concerned.

Notice also a related point: Sin never identifies itself as such. Sin does everything it can to camouflage itself. Satan wants you to focus on the fruit, not on the bigger picture of the meaning of life, eternity, or your

---

28 C.S. Lewis, *The Screwtape Letters* (New York, NY: HarperCollins, 2001), 60-61.

daily relationship with God. Sin hides in places where it thinks you'll never look. The big sins are made to appear as small as possible, and the little sins are made to look like righteousness by comparison. In our world the most horrific of sins mask themselves as "freedom of choice." Our culture packages and markets its belief that "there are no absolutes" as a humble tolerance of other cultures. Everyone is right and so no one is right, and we can all do as we please, bobbing blissfully adrift in an endless sea without any need for the high ground of moral or intellectual absolutes. The only absolute we will allow is the absolute that there are no absolutes, and only a brainwashed fanatic would dare suggest otherwise! Like a wolf in sheep's clothing, evil lurks everywhere under the pleasant-sounding banners of "freedom," "rights," and "tolerance."[29]

Sin is a trap; the bait is something small and good, and to work its magic on you, it must get you to focus on the bait and ignore the larger context. Satan uses the smallest of things to lure us in and destroy us. Think for a minute about the stupid things we waste our time on. My grandparents' generation spent most of their time sitting on the porch watching cars go by; personally, I could never figure out the appeal of such a thing. Think of the multitude of people who have wasted their lives focused on collecting baseball cards or stamps or vacation souvenirs to excess. I had a grandmother who invested a tremendous amount of energy into a collection of decorative ceramic shoes, of all things. They all went straight into the dumpster when she died. We try to amass this kind of rubbish seemingly to give us a sense of control in an uncontrollable world, to give us some sense of mastery and security and stability, but this is a wasted effort; true stability and security can be found only in God (cf. Isa 33.6; Mt 6.25-34).

---

29 I have sometimes thought that perhaps we should worry more about the pop singer singing pleasantly about the world's goods than the heavy metal screamer proclaiming himself evil. At least the screamer has the decency to tell you, in his especially candid way, that he's lying to you. The attractive pop star is much more likely to pull one over on you.

Think of the trillions upon trillions of hours invested in TV, and think of how little there will be to show for it when the dust settles. At least the gamer has an acute sense of how much time he wastes each day; the TV watcher generally has no sense of it at all. People are quick to talk about video game addiction but almost never about TV addiction. For some inexplicable reason, television has turned a blind eye to television addiction. The Dr. Phil episode about talk show addiction has been postponed indefinitely. Ask yourself this question: out of the thousands of TV episodes you have probably watched, how many of them did you any spiritual good? Was it time well spent for Jesus? Did you grow closer to God because of it, or was it completely and sinfully squandered? Consider the golfer, the model train enthusiast, the fantasy football player, and the Facebook addict. Consider also the words of Watson:

> *The world is like a shadow that declines. It is delightful, but deceitful; it promises more than we find, and it fails us when we have the most need of it. All the world [brings] changes and is constant only in its disappointments...The world is not a filling but a fleeting comfort...Why are we discontented at the loss of these things? Only because we expect that from them which is not, and depend on them for that which we ought not.*[30]

We don't need physical idols to worship; we don't need illicit sex and illegal drugs to waste our lives; we can make an idol of anything. We can be addicted to anything. The more socially acceptable the better as far as sin is concerned. Yet none of these things actually satisfy:

> *The world has an inconsolable longing. It tries to satisfy the longing with scenic vacations, accomplishments of creativity, stunning cinematic productions, sexual exploits, sports extravaganzas,*

30 Thomas Watson, *The Art of Divine Contentment* (Grand Rapids, MI: Soli Deo Gloria Publications, 2011), 125-126.

> *hallucinogenic drugs, ascetic rigors, managerial excellence, etcetera, etcetera. But the longing remains...The tragedy of the world is that the echo is mistaken for the Original Shout. When our back is to the breathtaking beauty of God we cast a shadow on the earth and fall in love with it. But it does not satisfy.*[31]

Understand this: The point is not that hobbies and entertainment are evil. The next two chapters will illustrate better that the world is not evil; the world is good. The point rather is that hobbies and entertainment can be used in sinful ways. Murder and cards are the same, so long as the end is the second death.[32]

It gets worse. Before we can begin to see some light at the end of this dark tunnel, we must go just a bit deeper, so bear with me another moment. If sin can't make us do the wrong thing, "plan B" is to make us do the right thing in the wrong way. We can make idols out of the very best of things. No doubt there have been many who spent their whole lives engulfed in studying their Bibles, but because it was not out of a sincere hope in Jesus or a sincere desire to honor God, but from some other motive—pride among their peers, being a local celebrity, parental acceptance, whatever—it was all just sin and they will end up in hell. Fifty years ago, pastor, writer, and counselor Martyn Lloyd-Jones spoke these very bleak words:

> *Have you ever seen a man like that facing the end of his life? Have you seen him when he can no longer read, or when he is on his deathbed? I have seen one or two and I do not want to see another. It is a terrible thing when a man reaches that point when he knows that he must die, and the gospel which he has argued about and reasoned about and 'defended' does not seem*

31 John Piper, *Desiring God: Meditations of a Christian Hedonist* (Portland, OR: Moltnomah, 1986), 214. By "Shout" and "echo," Piper just means that we mistake the creation for the Creator.

32 i.e., hell. See Revelation 20.14.

> *to help him because it has never gripped him. It was just an intellectual hobby.*[33]

Even many pastors and purported miracle-workers will hone their crafts for false motives, and Jesus will renounce knowing them (Mt 7.22-23). It will be discovered that they used their "Christianity" only as a means of furthering some other idolatrous pursuit. Our minds are incomprehensibly dark:

> *The heart is deceitful above all things,*
> *and desperately sick;*
> *who can understand it? (Jer 17.9)*

Self-deception is the worst kind of deception, since you carry the deceiver always with you.[34] We are world worshipers. We worship the shadow instead of the reality, the effect rather than the cause, the carnal[35] creature rather than the Spirit Creator. We worship ourselves; we worship others; we worship things. We're so addicted to sin that no sinner has ever been able (or will ever be able) to shake the habit (1 Jn 1.8). We are dense and blockish; we laugh at the stupid things we see other people addicted to—the button collector, the "Dead-head," and the "Trekkie" alike—since we know their idols are trivial. Yet when those pretentious smiles are cast in our direction and shine a condescending light on our worldly interests, we are wounded and must pridefully bolster our conviction that "this-thing-here is the real deal, even if all these ignorant peons don't see it." God will not need to condemn us; we will condemn ourselves; our own inconsistencies will bear witness against us; we will be judged by the standard with which we judged others (Mt 7.2). How

---

33 D. Martyn Lloyd-Jones, *Spiritual Depression: It's Causes and Cure* (Grand Rapids, MI: Wm. B. Eerdmans, 1965), 57.

34 This phrase was stolen, I believe, from Augustine, who stole it from Plato, who stole it from Socrates, who probably stole it from someone else.

35 "carnal" is synonymous with "fleshly" (i.e., physical things).

many will not awake from this slumber of entertainment and hobby until they find they have become tinder and the opportunity to change their mind has passed them by? We shudder in fear when our idols forsake us, not recognizing what is really fearful:

> *And so it is also with the natural man, he is ignorant of what the dreadful truly is, yet he is not thereby exempted from shuddering; no, he shudders at that which is not the dreadful: he does not know the true God, but this is not the whole of it, he worships an idol as God.*[36]

Consider the billionaire looking to make just a bit more, even though he cannot spend what he has. He no longer thinks of money in terms of utility. He no longer thinks of what good it can do or what he can buy with it. He pursues it as an end in itself. The numbers are imaginary, disconnected from any tangible reality. His thirst is never quenched; he is always seeking but never finding. When he dies, it will have all been for nothing; someone else will squander his fortune (cf. Lk 12.16-21).

Consider the teenager whose life is centered on finding love. Having not found their "soulmate"[37] yet, they remain in perpetual despair. The teenager's notion of romantic love is deceitful and idealized to its core. Their worship is directed at a fiction of their own imagination. They expect to find someone who will pursue their satisfaction with relentless,

---

36 Søren Kierkegaard, *The Sickness Unto Death* (Princeton, NJ: Princeton University Press, 1941), 8.

37 The idea of a "soulmate" is as vain a concept as ever the world conceived, when judged by a biblical standard. It seems to first appear in Plato's *Symposium*. It is nothing but crude, ancient mythology (https://en.wikipedia.org/wiki/Soulmate). We might consider throwing it into the pit along with our culture's concept of "falling in love" as well, or at least turning it upside down and giving it a hard shake to see if anything true falls out of it. The Bible doesn't speak of "falling in love," it only speaks of committing and covenanting to love. In the context of the Bible, love looks more like a settled decision than, as we tend to envision it, a pleasant emotion, subject always to change or revision.

everlasting zeal and total self-sacrifice, but will be surprised to find that whoever they meet will probably be just as sinfully self-absorbed as they are. In the end there will be two selfish people each demanding the other to not be selfish. Deceitful desires are eager to provide a faulty perspective on love and a faulty foundation for social relationships.

Consider the Facebooker, meditating the day away coming up with witty memes and one-liners. How could so many words add up to so little, when it takes only one word to condemn an entire generation? "When words are many, transgression is not lacking, but whoever restrains his lips is prudent" (Pr 10.19).

Think also of the pride—the self-worship—that is common to all of us. One *Washington Post* poll revealed that 44% of young Americans (18–24) believed they were going to be famous, at least for a short time, while 60% of those in their later twenties believed the same.[38] We all seem to believe that any day now the world will come to see and understand our surpassing merits and inherent worth, and we will be the recipients of its endless praise. We have been taught that the lack of self-esteem is at the root of all of our problems, and we seem to have been taught too well, because while we are spiritually useless, we value ourselves quite highly. One popular film has it at least partly right:

> *Advertising has us chasing cars and clothes, working jobs we hate so we can buy [stuff!] we don't need. We're the middle children of history...No purpose or place. We have no Great War. No Great Depression. Our great war is a spiritual war. Our great depression is our lives. We've all been raised on television to believe that one day we'd all be millionaires, and movie gods, and rock stars, but we won't. We're slowly learning that fact.*

---

38 Richard Morin, "Famous for 15 Minutes," *Wastington Post*, last modified August 28, 2000, accessed July 28, 2012, http://www.washingtonpost.com/wp-srv/politics/polls/wat/archive/wat082800.htm

> *And we're very, very [upset!].*[39]

The delusion of the young is a prideful optimism; the delusion of the old is they believe they have come to know better. Kierkegaard pointed out that older adults often look at their past selves and think that, even though they used to be naïve, they have now arrived at all knowledge:

> *People overlook the fact that illusion has essentially two forms; that of hope, and that of recollection...The older man is not plagued by the illusion of hope, but he is on the other hand by the whimsical idea of looking down at the illusion of youth from a supposedly superior standpoint which is free from illusion. The youth is under illusion, he hopes for the extraordinary from life and from himself. By way of [comparison] one often finds in an older man illusion with respect to the recollections of his youth.*[40]

We think of worship as an event where people fall flat on the ground and mutter repetitive spiritual formulas. We see the action play out in our minds, but we miss the meaning of it. The bowing down is not what's important—it's the meaning behind it. You bow down to signify the exultation of whatever it is to which you bow down. Bowing down is an act of praise indicating "I am very low, and you are very high." If you want to know what you worship, look at what you praise, what you enjoy talking about, what you throw your money at, what you hold high and want others to hold high alongside you. Where your treasure is, there your heart will be (Mt 6.21). Out of the abundance of the heart, the mouth speaks (Mt 12.34). "All enjoyment," said C.S. Lewis, "spontaneously overflows into praise."[41] Worship is man's natural state. Worship

---

39 *Fight Club*, directed by David Fincher (1999; 20th Century Fox, 2000), DVD.

40 Søren Kierkegaard, *The Sickness Unto Death* (Princeton, NJ: Princeton University Press, 1941), 65.

41 C.S. Lewis, quoted in John Piper, *Desiring God: Meditations of a Christian*

happens for every person, every day. That is what we were designed to do, at the very core of what we *are*. We cannot *not* worship. Worshiping is as natural for us as breathing. The fundamental sin of man is not that he has failed to worship, but that he has committed himself to worship *anything but* God. We're addicted to earthly things; we worship our appetites; our god is our belly:

> *Their end is destruction, their god is their belly, and they glory in their shame, with minds set on earthly things. But our citizenship is in heaven, and from it we await a Savior, the Lord Jesus Christ. (Phil 3.19-20)*

The apostles speak frequently of the "world's desires" and "worldliness" and the like, but often they don't tell us precisely what sin they are referring to. This is because we can set our affection on anything. Any definition which included particular sins would miss the whole point that "worldliness" can take an infinite number of forms. We can turn our desires toward any object under the sun. Some people pursue primarily just one idol, whereas most people focus on many. Sin would rather we have many idols so that no one of them draws attention to itself and becomes too obvious. Sin's work in us is utterly deceptive; when we set our hope and our happiness and our joy on *things* and we seek our satisfaction therein, we are asking those things to do for us what they were not designed to do. It's bound to end in frustration, like trying to drive a coffee pot to work. It simply cannot go well, neither in this life nor in eternity. By the very definition of it, it will end in failure. As a result, the world is filled with an inconsolable longing. The sports fan covets a championship team, but even if his wish is fulfilled, it will not meet his expectations. It will leave emptiness in its wake. The one investing their hope in money will never have enough. The one seeking fame for fame's sake will not like it if he happens to stumble upon it. The one seeking

---

Hedonist (Portland, OR: Moltnomah, 1986), 17.

sex in the wrong places can never be satisfied. We are always hoping but never attaining, always running but never arriving.

What is it that enslaves you? What is it that your wallet is always wide open to? What is it that your happiness is contingent upon, and you're always quick to defend when others question your level of commitment to it? It seems that all sin is something like alcohol consumption: the more you drink, the thirstier you are, the more invincible you feel, and the more blurred your vision becomes. Yet, in truth, your situation becomes more precarious with each drink.[42]

We should also stop at least once more to rubberneck at the train wreck of video game addiction. With gaming, under the surface, what is there of substance? No matter how good the game, the experience is ultimately bound to be shallow and repetitive. Someone has coded a world for me, outside of which I can do nothing. I can neither add to nor subtract from the world I am placed in. The game's creator establishes the boundaries. My same experience, individual though I like to think it, is repeated by a million others. Each player navigates the path the developer has plotted, and reaches the same conclusions at roughly the same rate. The plots are almost always half-baked and formulaic. The game is addictive not by consequence but by design. It is designed—as is all entertainment media—not for my happiness and well-being, but to enslave me for someone else's profit. They have supplied an endless number of objectives, goals, points, trophies, whatever, to keep me perpetually winning. The game is perfectly balanced to make me feel like a person who knows how to overcome great adversity, while in reality everything is geared toward my victory; every game is designed to win. Only the worst of players will actually get stuck. The game developer doesn't benefit by frustrating players, and the game has to satisfy the six-year-old just as well as it satisfies the forty-year-old. A death in the game is a minor setback, marked by a checkpoint, on the road to

42 The diligent reader could infer my view on alcohol from chapters 8 and 9.

certain victory. The perceived challenge is, in large measure, a fiction.

Especially in role-playing games, it becomes obvious at times that it's not so much that the game is satisfying *right now, as* we hope it *will be* satisfying when we get to such-and-such a point or own such-and-such an item. The truth, however, is that once we get to that point, we don't *actually* just kick back and enjoy our accomplishments, but rather it's another hundred hours of grinding to get to the next little carrot. We try to fill games with more meaning than they merit. We try not to think about the time invested and the poor dividend we've received. We try not to think about the fact that none of these trails of little carrots has ever led us to anything of lasting significance. We are forced to stop frequently to assure ourselves that it will probably be different this time than it has been every other time. When hobbies rise to a sinful level, you will always find that you never *actually* arrived at the satisfaction you anticipated, for such is the nature of sin. This is our deceitful desires at work.

At least be honest with yourself. You'll never be the best. There will always be some mildly autistic savant who you can't possibly compete with. There will always be someone hacking, cheating, botting, and exploiting to gain an unfair advantage. There will always be someone with better equipment, better peripherals, and a better internet connection. There will always be some no-lifer willing to put in more time, energy, and dedication than you. And, let's face it, carpal tunnel and "computer elbow" are just around the bend for all of us.

Games are a wonderful distraction from life's troubles and that's it. That's all they are and all that they can be. Yet online game forums seem filled to the brim with angry customers talking like the fate of the world is at stake. We demand faster updates and better endgame. We demand that developers purge the sadness from our spirits with more and better "content."

In those moments when I would question the time I was investing into video games, I would sometimes ask myself what I liked so much about them. I came to the conclusion that players long primarily for the learning curve. It's the process of constant discovery. It's the next car, the next weapon, the next suit of armor, the next level, the next cutscene, the next quest, the endless discovery of the unknown. The game maker hangs the carrot in front of the player's noses and promises that there are great things to come to those who reach the goal—fame and glory and honor. Yet, ultimately, they cannot keep this promise. When you reach the proposed destination, you discover merely another carrot to pursue. Every game is self-contained; it can never offer anything beyond itself. To a great extent, we encourage game developers to make big promises they can't keep, because we want those promises to be true. We all want, with everything in us, to be satisfied.

We have disconnected ourselves from God, and we make up the rules as we go. We try to define ourselves and our meaning without reference to God. We are left, therefore, seeking depth in places where there is no depth. We seek meaning in the fruit rather than in God. We follow our appetites; we interpret things how we want to.[43] Do not be foolish. Listen to John and be wise:

---

43 Natural science is always claiming to interpret the "hard data" and "facts" of nature objectively and without bias, but this view is philosophically laughable. The hard data used to prove that the world was flat and that the sun revolved around the earth. The theory of evolution, for example, is an overarching, all-encompassing filter through which every fact passes. The evolutionist doesn't ask *if* some creatures are millions of years old, but rather *which ones*, because his system itself demands that some, if not all, species be millions of years old. The conclusion is known before the facts are ever examined, for the system is read into the facts. Every good scientist admits that every scientific theory is always subject to revision, and in a thousand years, scientists will undoubtedly think about the world much differently than they do now. Don't build your house upon such shifting sand. The world claims certainty about such things only to console itself in the face of a more certain Judgment. (cf. Lk 2.25) See my book *Evolution Evolves (which was written subsequent to this one)*, in which I explore the vanity and futility of the system of atheistic evolution.

> *Do not love the world or the things in the world. If anyone loves the world, the love of the Father is not in him. For all that is in the world—the desires of the flesh and the desires of the eyes and pride of life—is not from the Father but is from the world. And the world is passing away along with its desires, but whoever does the will of God abides forever. (I Jn 2.15-17)*

Listen to the wisdom of the Puritans:

> *If you [want to] get a contented life, do not grasp too much of the world, do not take in more of the business of the world than God calls you to. Do not be greedy of taking in a great deal of the world, for if a man goes among thorns, when he may take a simpler way, he has no reason to complain that he is pricked with them...If men and women will thrust themselves on things of the world which they do not need, then no wonder that they are pricked and meet with what disturbs them. For such is the nature of all things here in this world... We will meet with disappointments and discontentments in everything we meddle with.*[44]

The things of this world were not intended to fulfill our deepest emotional needs. They simply cannot. To all perfection, I see an end, a limit to its power to satisfy man. Contrast this with the reality of knowing the infinite God:

> *Can you find out the deep things of God?*
> *Can you find out the limit of the Almighty?*
> *It is higher than heaven—what can you do?*
> *Deeper than Sheol—what can you know?*
> *Its measure is longer than the earth and broader than the sea.*
> *(Job 11.7-9)*

---

44 Jeremiah Burroughs, *The Rare Jewel of Christian Contentment* (1648; repr., Carlisle, PA: The Banner of Truth Trust, 2009), 216.

We were not created for creature worship. We were not designed to be satisfied by the things of this world. The things of this world are intended only as tools to make us draw near to God. Their inappropriate use is doomed to be unsatisfactory to us, for they were never intended to satisfy the deepest needs of our soul. We were not designed to be awed by the finite but by the infinite, and there is an infinite gap between the two. Unlike the learning curve of games, the learning curve of knowing Jesus never ends:

> *Has not God given you Christ? In Him there are unsearchable riches. He is such a gold mine of wisdom and grace that all the saints and angels can never dig to the bottom...He is an enriching pearl, a sparkling diamond. The infinite luster of His merits makes us shine in God's eyes. In Him there is both fullness and sweetness; He is indescribably good. Lift up your thoughts to the highest pinnacle; stretch them to the utmost; let them wander to their full latitude and extent—yet they fall infinitely short of those ineffable and inexhaustible treasures which are locked up in Jesus Christ. And is there not enough here to give the soul contentment? A Christian who lacks necessities, yet, having Christ, has the one thing needful.*[45]

45 Thomas Watson. *The Art of Divine Contentment*, (1653; repr., Grand Rapids, MI: Soli Deo Gloria Publications, 2011), 70.

8

WHEN DOES LIBERTY BECOME IDOLATRY?

Another question I had plenty of time to think about was *how do you know if a particular hobby is wrong?* The Bible clearly prohibits certain activities, but what about the multitude of activities about which it says nothing? What is the Bible's position on Facebook, on video games, on R-rated movies? Is it absurd for us to ask God's ancient book questions about today's modern technology? Should we instead simply rest on our own intuitions and throw about our own opinions *ad nauseam*? Here I would suggest that if we truly believe the Bible to be God's revelation (i.e., revealing) of himself to man, we should have at least some suspicion that the Bible is forward-thinking enough to lay out some general principles which are perfectly relevant today. After all, we have already seen that the perfection of God's word surpasses every earthly thing and that it is boundless—more than sufficient to meet our every need.

The Apostle Paul, in his letter to the Christians in Rome, lays out what have come to be known as the principles of "Christian Liberty." The death and resurrection of Jesus sent a shock wave through the ancient world which is still felt today. Rome was the hub of the ancient world, the center of trade and culture, and, as one might expect, Christianity took root early there.[46] The church there, not surprisingly, was composed

46 cf. William Hendriksen, *New Testament Commentary: Romans* (Grand

of both Jews and Gentiles. Many in that congregation had been raised under Old Testament Judaism with all its ceremonial regulations, food restrictions, and complex sacrificial system, while others were Gentiles who grew up with an eclectic polytheism. The Pulitzer prize-winning historian Will Durant describes the religion native to Rome as:

> *a polymorphous mass of popular belief in animism, fetishism, totemism, magic, miracles, spells, superstitions, and taboos... Amulets were well-nigh universal; nearly every child wore a... golden talisman, suspended from his neck. Small images were hung upon doors or trees to ward off evil spirits. Charms or incantations were used to avert accidents, cure disease, bring rain, destroy a hostile army, wither an enemy's crops or [the enemy] himself.*[47]

In light of this clash of diverse and sometimes superstitious cultures, it's no surprise that the Christians in Rome questioned what was acceptable for the Christian and what wasn't. Not surprisingly, the first question that came up seems to have been regarding that most fundamental of human needs: food.

The New Testament talks about food a great deal. To the contemporary chubby American, who never goes without, this can be a bit puzzling, but we have to keep a few things in mind. First, we have to understand that the persecution of Christians from all sides had already begun. It was becoming increasingly difficult to function in society without participating in one form of idolatry or another. People were commonly cut off from employment or refused service at the market, and the level of hunger was clearly high among these early Christians. When your belly is empty, you're much less likely to ask questions about

---

Rapids, MI, 2004), 15-23.

47 Will Durant, *The Story of Civilization: Part 3: Caesar and Christ* (New York, NY: Simon and Schuster, 1944), 60.

the morality of eating this rather than that, and so questions about food were very pressing.

A second thing to keep in mind is that where Christ deemed all foods clean (Mark 7:19), the Jews who rejected Christ (and even some who accepted him) continued to maintain the old restrictions against pork and other foods that were considered ceremonially unclean. So the question was natural, should certain foods still be avoided to accommodate such opinions? Will abstaining from bacon somehow make me more holy?

A final thing to remember is that it was common practice in the ancient gentile world to dedicate (or "sacrifice") your meal to one of the local gods (usually via your household idol or representation of that god) before you ate it. To the gentile converts, the natural question was, is a Christian prohibited from eating a meal that has been offered to an idol? We know gods carved out of wood aren't really gods, after all, so does it *really* make any difference?

Paul offers a few simple principles, which we would be wise to examine. Before we do that, however, we have to stop to note that Paul's discussion of Christian liberty is grounded upon his understanding of what it is to be a Christian. Let me offer a very brief outline of Paul's understanding of what it is to be a Christian, which he lays out in the first few chapters of the letter to the Romans: we are all born under the law, which is to say that God requires perfect obedience of every person. God is perfectly holy and, as to moral choices, God holds man to the same standard to which he holds himself, namely, perfection. However, all men fall short of this standard in some measure, and all are therefore fit for the punishment of hell. God himself, however, mercifully intervened. God the Father sent his only Son into the world to extract man out of this ugly predicament. Jesus perfectly obeyed all the commandments, yet he died the death of a sinner in our place. He took our punishment for us, satisfied God's perfect sense of justice through his righteous sacrifice, and we get his righteousness through faith. Though he was *actually* sinless, Jesus was *legally* accounted as sinful in our place for a time, so that we who are *actually* sinful could be accounted *legally* righteous in league with him forever. All who trust in him are no longer under the law of works since they are already deemed righteous, but rather they enter into a new relationship with God which Paul calls a relationship of grace. Because we have total forgiveness in Christ through faith, there is no longer any chance of our condemnation. Our past, present, and future sins have been forgiven forever, and our good standing before God is not based on our personal righteousness, but rather on the righteousness of Christ. Therefore, under grace, God is no longer a strict judge to be feared, but a loving Father to be honored. Under the law, we were slaves to sin and its deceitful desires, but under grace, we are free to pursue all good things in Christ without fear, having our eyes opened to the fact that sin is a slave driver that never truly satisfies us or lives up to its own promises. Keeping this context in mind, we will spend this chapter and the following looking at this passage from Paul's letter. Read carefully:

> *I know and am persuaded in the Lord Jesus that nothing is unclean in itself, but it is unclean for anyone who thinks it unclean. For if your brother is grieved by what you eat, you are no longer walking in love. By what you eat, do not destroy the one for whom Christ died. So do not let what you regard as good be spoken of as evil. For the kingdom of God is not a matter of eating and drinking but of righteousness and peace and joy in the Holy Spirit. Whoever thus serves Christ is acceptable to God and approved by men. So then let us pursue what makes for peace and for mutual upbuilding.*
>
> *Do not, for the sake of food, destroy the work of God. Everything is indeed clean, but it is wrong for anyone to make another stumble by what he eats. It is good not to eat meat or drink wine or do anything that causes your brother to stumble. The faith that you have, keep between yourself and God. Blessed*

> *is the one who has no reason to pass judgment on himself for what he approves. But whoever has doubts is condemned if he eats, because the eating is not from faith. For whatever does not proceed from faith is sin.*
>
> *We who are strong have an obligation to bear with the failings of the weak, and not to please ourselves. Let each of us please his neighbor for his good, to build him up. For Christ did not please himself, but as it is written, "The reproaches of those who reproached you fell on me." For whatever was written in former days was written for our instruction, that through endurance and through the encouragement of the Scriptures we might have hope. May the God of endurance and encouragement grant you to live in such harmony with one another, in accord with Christ Jesus, that together you may with one voice glorify the God and Father of our Lord Jesus Christ. Therefore welcome one another as Christ has welcomed you, for the glory of God. (Rom 14.14–5.7)*

While talking about food in particular, Paul lays out several general principles for Christians to use for all matters that may be unclear. This is fantastic guidance for those many grey areas of life and deserves real reflection. Lying, stealing, and extramarital sex may be clear enough issues, obviously prohibited throughout the Bible, but what about music, movies, video games, wardrobe preferences, the internet, and countless other areas the Bible does not specifically address? Paul gives us the answers to all of those questions here. I think we can safely derive four general principles from this passage:

1. *Anything not specifically prohibited by the Bible, either directly or indirectly, is acceptable in itself.*

2. *Even though everything is acceptable in itself, not every person will have the same tolerance for everything.*

3. *If what you judge to be okay for you causes another person to sin, you are not honoring the biblical command to love your neighbor.*

4. *The glory of God must be central in everything in our lives.*

Let's start with the first.

1. **Anything not specifically prohibited by the Bible, either directly or indirectly, is acceptable in itself.**

Paul says simply that "nothing is unclean in itself" (14.14). Our Lord himself likewise said the same thing several times:

> *And he called the people to him again and said to them, "Hear me, all of you, and understand: There is nothing outside a person that by going into him can defile him, but the things that come out of a person are what defile him." And when he had entered the house and left the people, his disciples asked him about the parable. And he said to them, "Then are you also without understanding? Do you not see that whatever goes into a person from outside cannot defile him, since it enters not his heart but his stomach, and is expelled?" (Thus he declared all foods clean.) And he said, "What comes out of a person is what defiles him. For from within, out of the heart of man, come evil thoughts, sexual immorality, theft, murder, adultery, coveting, wickedness, deceit, sensuality, envy, slander, pride, foolishness. All these evil things come from within, and they defile a person." (Mk 7.14–23)*[48]

Jesus was specifically speaking of eating certain meats, but it's clear the apostles understood this to apply to all other areas of life. It's not what goes in that makes a man wicked, but what comes out from his heart. Wasn't Jesus himself often spotted sitting among sinners? Is it

48 See also Mt. 15:10–20

not certain that he overheard all manner of sinful dialogues and that he witnessed innumerable types of sinful activity unfolding before him at one time or another? Does contact with impurity somehow make Jesus a sinner? No, because the person who is pure processes everything in a way that is pure:

> *To the pure, all things are pure, but to the defiled and unbelieving, nothing is pure; but both their minds and their consciences are defiled. They profess to know God, but they deny him by their works. They are detestable, disobedient, unfit for any good work. (Tit 1.15)*

Just as Jesus could be in the presence of wickedness and still come away pure, the evil person, by contrast, can sit and listen to the most glorious and pleasant of sermons and still process it in a way that is wicked. The Pharisees listened to Jesus' pleasant, objectively beautiful, objectively glorious and life-changing words, while internally they were plotting to kill him. The corrupt person is incapable of doing any good work whatsoever. He is, as Paul explains, "unfit for any good work" because his motive is always worldly. He does not care about pleasing God in anything he does.

It seems then that the problem is not in the things of this world, but rather the problem is in *us*. If a man sees a woman and lusts after her, we wouldn't suppose the cause of the lust was somehow in the woman, but rather it goes without saying that, with respect to the lust, the problem is in the man. The problem is obviously not the mere existence of women; the problem is rather that men look at women in a way in which God did not originally intend. Here is a simple principle: *Just because people abuse something doesn't mean that thing is evil.* We Americans abuse food every day; does that make food evil? Let's hope not. We abuse language; does that make language evil? Any argument against language in general, without using some sort of language, is going to prove difficult to convey. We abuse our eyes by looking at what we should not, our hands by doing what we should not, our feet by going where we should not. As a general rule, we are perfect in nothing, and, therefore, we abuse every*thing*, every day, at least a little bit. Our sin is heavier than we are generally willing to acknowledge. We have absolutely no hope at all of obeying God's law perfectly, a fact which should always lead us back to the hope of forgiveness found in the cross and the gospel ("good news") of Jesus Christ.

So the problem is not with the things God has given us. The problem is just the way we use them. We can easily apply this principle to our own daily lives. As simple as it is, still it has far-reaching consequences in the life of the believer. Take the internet, for example. A lot of evil happens there. Recent statistics suggest it's nearly 40% pornographic sites, and 200 are added each and every day.[49] All manner of criminal activity happens online through the World Wide Web, all hastened by anonymity and the privacy and comfort of one's own home. On the other hand, does God use the internet for his purposes? Have people become Christians through the internet? Is there uplifting content out there? Of course! It is, obviously, one of the most powerful educational tools in human history, perhaps bested only by books. So can we offer a blanket condemnation of the internet? Of course not.

We must not lose sight of the fact that everything God made is good.[50] Our abuse of food does not mean food is bad. Our abuse of the internet does not mean the internet is bad. Our abuse of movies does not make movies bad. Our abuse of video games does not mean video games are bad. This is not at all to say that every internet activity, movie, and video game is acceptable, however. In order to see the big picture, we have three more principles to review.

---

49 Richard Winter, *Still Bored in a Culture of Entertainment* (Downer Grove, IL: Intervarsity Press, 2002), 105.

50 This includes things humans create from the elements of God's creation, like technology, art, etc.

9

WHEN DOES LIBERTY BECOME UNPROFITABLE?

There is a second principle Paul offers in Romans 14:

2. **Even though everything is acceptable in itself, not every person will have the same tolerance for everything.**

Nothing is unclean in itself, but it is unclean to the person who cannot use it without sinning. We must judge for ourselves whether we are able to use each thing responsibly and uprightly. Paul says simply that, even though nothing is unclean in itself, still it "is unclean for anyone who thinks it unclean" (14.14). This sounds very subjective for a divinely inspired author, especially an adamant and unbending person like Paul, but the principle is again straightforward. Returning to the easy example of the internet, we concluded that there is nothing inherently wrong with having the internet in one's home, but is that to say it's okay for everyone? What about the bachelor who, no matter how hard he tries, cannot stop looking at internet pornography every day? Would he be wise to get rid of his internet and just use the internet at the nearest library when he needs to?

But put on the Lord Jesus Christ, and make no provision for the flesh, to gratify its desires. (Rom 13.14)

If isolating yourself away from the internet will make your struggle easier, if removing the source of temptation will give you the upper hand in your battle against sin, then don't hesitate. Get right to the very root and cut it off there! Make no provision for the flesh; provide nothing to that old sinner inside of you; cut off every source of his sustenance and starve him until he is dead. Take off your old self, and put on a brand new self (Eph 4.22-24). Pulling the plug on your computer, your TV, your cell phone, or your video game console is an appalling and obscene notion to the social media generation, but this goes right to the heart of refusing to conform to the world's standards (Rom 12.2), right to the heart of making God your central concern. Are we serious about this Christian life or not? If not, then eat, drink, and be merry, for tomorrow we die (1 Cor 15.32; also Lk 12.9). If so, then consider the appalling, brutal, and decisive words of Jesus:

If your right eye causes you to sin, tear it out and throw it away. For it is better that you lose one of your members than that your whole body be thrown into hell. And if your right hand causes you to sin, cut it off and throw it away. For it is better that you lose one of your members than that your whole body go into hell. (Mt 5.29-30)

You must judge for yourself, given your own circumstances, whether a thing is acceptable for you. Be decisive. If, after a time of thought, you find you are still hesitating as to whether that thing is okay for you or not, that thing is sin for you. Get rid of it, at least temporarily, until you are in a better position to make an objective and God-centered decision. Paul says simply, "whoever has doubts is condemned if he eats" (14.23). Talk of being condemned in the context of the Bible is not to be taken lightly.

In contrast, "Blessed is the one who has no reason to pass judgment on himself for what he approves" (14.22). As we will see later, a possible alternative translation of "blessed" is "very happy." The Christian who knows how to use each thing appropriately, knows how to be thankful to God for everything, and knows how to use everything to help him become a better Christian is blessed indeed. The life in pursuit of deceitful desires is a life of slavery, but the Christian life is a life of liberty. "For freedom Christ has set us free; stand firm, therefore, and do not submit again to a yoke of slavery" (Gal 5:1).

With regard to your particular area of concern, here are the questions you need to ask yourself: Am I using this sinfully? Has this hobby interfered with my relationship with God and others? Do I seek to get from this thing what I should seek to get from God? If any of these are true and you find you are perpetually doubting whether you are pursuing that activity appropriately, here is your answer, I will tell you plainly: your continued use of that thing is a sin; it is an instance of world worship to be torn down. Pull the plug; act decisively. Take a good long break to clear your head. There is zero chance you will ever regret that decision.

There is a third principle in Romans 14:

3. **If what you judge to be okay for you causes another person to sin, you are not honoring the biblical command to love your neighbor.**

Paul says, "for if your brother is grieved by what you eat, you are no longer walking in love. By what you eat, do not destroy the one for whom Christ died" (14.15). Perhaps you conclude that your relationship with God is not being ill-affected by the liberty you've chosen to take with this or that particular interest or pursuit. Is someone else being negatively affected by your decision? Are you leading your family down the right path and proving yourself to be a good example, or is it having a negative spiritual impact on your family and other close relationships? Paul concludes, "let us pursue what makes for peace and for mutual upbuilding" (14.19) and "Everything is indeed clean, but it is wrong for anyone to make another stumble by what he eats" (14.20). Not only should your liberty not cause you to stumble away from the narrow road, it shouldn't cause anyone else to stumble either.[51] In his letter to the Christians in Corinth, Paul is even more direct to this point, responding to the person who grabs hold of the first principle at the expense of all of the others:

> *"All things are lawful," but not all things are helpful. "All things are lawful," but not all things build up. (I Cor 10.23)*

Christian liberty oversteps its boundaries at the point where it doesn't build up the believer himself or his brothers and sisters. Paul encourages discretion in this regard: "The faith that you have, keep between yourself and God"(14.22). You might find some R-rated movies, for instance, acceptable for yourself; there's no need to advertise it or to push them on others who could be more sensitive to such content. Exercising discretion is not a form of lying. Discretion springs simply from the understanding that not everything is for everyone.

"You, my brothers and sisters," says Paul, "were called to be free. But do not use your freedom to indulge the flesh; rather, serve one another humbly in love. For the entire law is fulfilled in keeping this one command: 'Love your neighbor as yourself.'" (Gal 5.13-14)

There is a fourth and final principle; this is the highest of the bunch, the most challenging, the one that strikes hardest at the core of the issue and encompasses all of the others in itself.

---

51 To be clear, to cause a person to stumble means you are providing them an avenue of temptation. Drinking in front of a drunkard may cause stumbling, for instance (no pun intended!). On the other hand, if you should meet a legalist who says "the internet is bad in general, and I am offended by you having the internet," that is not causing them to stumble; that is just them being judgmental. That is their sin, and not yours. That is not what Paul is talking about.

4. The glory of God must be central in everything in our lives.

Whether we choose to eat or to not eat, to enjoy our liberty or to refrain, alongside our fellow Christians, we must "with one voice glorify the God and Father of our Lord Jesus Christ" (15.6). Paul is even clearer elsewhere. Shortly after he says "'All things are lawful,' but not all things are helpful. 'All things are lawful,' but not all things build up" (I Cor 10.23), he concludes:

> *So, whether you eat or drink, or whatever you do, do all to the glory of God. Give no offense to Jews or to Greeks or to the church of God, just as I try to please everyone in everything I do, not seeking my own advantage, but that of many, that they may be saved. (10.31-33)*

In every area of our life, it's hard to get by this one unscathed, without feeling convicted and condemned. We cannot but reckon ourselves failures when we compare ourselves to this standard and recognize our profound need for the forgiveness found in the cross. Say you have concluded that a particular pursuit is not inherently sinful (principle 1). Say you do not feel it is making you (principle 2) or anyone around you (principle 3) a worse Christian. Here is the next, more difficult question: "Do I do this thing in a way that glorifies God?" or "Does this thing make me a better Christian?" Whereas the first three principles ask us whether that thing is detrimental to our Christian success, this principle goes further, and Paul asks us if they are making us better Christians. Not only should *your hobbies not hurt you*, but they *should help* you in your Christianity. Every earthly thing was designed to lead us closer to God. All things are to be done to his glory. To the degree that they do not accomplish that end, they are, at best, a sinful waste of time. "The essence of sin, in other words," said Martyn Lloyd-Jones, "is that we do not live entirely to the glory of God."[52]

---

52 D. Martyn Lloyd-Jones, *Spiritual Depression: It's Causes and Cure* (Grand

Take video games again. It's entirely possible to play video games to the glory of God. Video games are art, at least in the ancient sense of the term.[53] With the budgets of many games now surpassing those of many Hollywood films, a tremendous amount of human thought and effort goes into each, and, just like Hollywood movies, many have redeeming qualities. We see in them scenes of power and glory, of righteousness and unrighteousness, of truth and falsehood, of beauty and ugliness, of mercy and justice, of wrath and grace—the entire range of what it is to be a human, made in the image of God but defiled by sin. The righteous man can benefit from them without a doubt. The imprint of God is stamped upon everything in this world, as in every work of art we see something of the artist, and so video games, like movies, point to God, often despite themselves. To the pure all things are pure.

At the same time, for myself I cannot but confess that I have fallen profoundly short of this high standard. Last year, I suspect I played video games probably thirty hours per week, say 1600 hours for the year, and during the same time period, I'm not sure I read a single book. My Bible reading was limited to Sunday morning church service, but not an hour passed without thinking about gaming. Weeks went by without a single prayer. I made a shipwreck of my faith; I traded eternal glory for temporal gain, and, as it turns out, my only temporal gain was a mild case of carpal tunnel syndrome.

Rapids, MI: Wm. B. Eerdmans, 1965), 31.

53 Basically anything produced by the hands of men—any Art-ifact—was considered Art in the ancient world, even things like pots and pans and woven baskets.

10

OUR GREATEST HAPPINESS

I remember in middle school, my well-intentioned youth pastor was trying to make the point that righteousness was objectively good and should be considered desirable. He posed the question like this: "Even if there were no God, wouldn't it be better to do good rather than evil? Isn't it better to work for something than to steal it, or to be nice to someone rather than to be cruel?" Something about this question seemed suspicious to me, perhaps even counterintuitive, and so, uncharacteristically, I raised my hand and was called on.

"If I knew God didn't exist, I don't think I would try to do good. I think I would just do whatever I could get away with," I said, no doubt with a bit of an arrogant grin.

The room chuckled a bit, and the youth pastor wasn't particularly pleased by this, so he put a little bit of social pressure on me. I have always had a bit of social anxiety, so he probably figured it wouldn't take much to get me to crack.

"So you're saying if there were no God, you'd live like a heathen?" he asked. Heathen! The King's English was not to be taken lightly in that church!

I hesitated. I needed a bit of reassurance now. In adolescent squeaks, I asked, "Now I'm certain, in this example, that there is no God?"

"That's right," he said.

I paused for a moment, and then responded, "Then yeah, what would be the point? I think I would just do whatever I could get away with."

His voice began to crackle a bit with fire and brimstone. "So you're saying you'd be a wicked heathen?"

The pressure grew more uncomfortable. I sought further reassurance of the terms. "There's no hell, right? No God? Nothing, right?"

"Right."

"Then yeah, I'd live however I wanted."

His tone changed to a high-pitched, polite form of condescension. "So if there's no God, no hell, you're telling me you're a heathen?" In a moment I went from being merely a rhetorical heathen to now being a present tense heathen. This was a clever rhetorical shift on his part.

The pressure was too much for me to continue, so I threw up my arms and proclaimed awkwardly, "I'm a heathen!"

The few chuckles in the room did not dissuade the youth pastor from continuing to make his point and bringing the class to a close.[54] Afterward, out in the hall, several peers told me covertly that they agreed with me.

I thought about that exchange for the next seventeen years or so, and during that time I agreed with myself completely. I now see, however, that I was dead wrong about one thing at least. Even though the question itself was somewhat misguided, still my position in the debate, as hypothetical heathen, said something about my deepest beliefs. What was I saying at bottom? What unconscious belief is implied in my answer? Among other things, I assumed that sin is, in itself, more satisfying than

---

54 Which point, in retrospect, seems somewhat misguided, since it posits a false dilemma and makes morality good just for morality's sake. Every pagan philosopher believes in morality for morality's sake. Satan himself loves when we are moral for morality's sake, because then morality itself becomes an idol, standing in the place of obedience to God.

righteousness. My answer betrayed the fact that I sincerely believed there was more pleasure to be found in sin than in righteousness in this life.

Thus we commonly find ourselves in a dual predicament. On the one hand, we tell ourselves the life of sin offers us the greatest possible satisfaction in this world, and we deem the Christian life to be a life of unhappy duty and sacrifice. On the other hand, we tell ourselves to forgo the life of sin in order to go to heaven, but we're not fully convinced heaven is actually worth the sacrifice. In the end, the formula for Christian success reads something like this: give up something good to gain something bad. Give up happiness on earth to gain a boring eternity.

When situations in my life had seemingly forced me to choose between the dedicated Christian life or the life of endless entertainment, I chose entertainment simply because I believed that there was more happiness to be found in entertainment than in the pursuit of God. I thought video games were the way to go, so, naturally, that's the way I went. The Christian life, I thought, was a life of sacrifice and of forgoing one's life now in order to gain eternal life. The life of sin is the really happy life, I thought. In light of these unfortunate facts of fallen human reality, the goal for each Christian is to take up his cross and focus as hard as he can on the goal of heaven. You just have to continually remind yourself the misery and boredom only last a little while, after which you will have the distinct pleasure of croaking and the eternal reward of singing hymns forever in a sort of endless and monotonous Sunday morning church service. The paradox, I thought, was that you have to give up this life to gain the next life. That's what Jesus said, isn't it? Forgo your happiness in this life to gain happiness in the next; give up temporal joy to gain eternal joy.[55] The trick to it all, the key that could unlock the universe, I

55 Culturally, we tend to think of "joy" as a spiritual concept, a sort of Godly satisfaction unaffected by various situations, and we tend to think of "happiness" as a more superficial sense of fun and pleasantness. (Therefore, given these definitions, the world cares deeply about being happy but isn't concerned much at all about joy.) Looking to the Bible, we don't find in it a

thought, was focusing on the next life almost exclusively, which always seemed like an impossible task in light of the endless fun to be had right now, right before your eyes, in sin.

So we come to the tough question—and it is indeed a tough question: Is it true? Does the Bible teach that the Christian life is an unhappy life in comparison with the life of sin? Now understand I am not talking about "in the grand scheme of things," nor am I talking about the next life. I am talking about your life right here, right now, this very moment, today. Can the things God made make you happier today than the God who made them? There is no third option here; either the life in pursuit of righteousness or the life in pursuit of sinful pleasures offers man the greatest potential for happiness right now. Both cannot be true, so it must be one or the other.

Let us look to the Bible. Let us pose the question to it and follow where it leads. Is sin really our happiest option today? Did sin so deform the world that man's greatest happiness is no longer found in God, but in sin? At the outset, we can certainly point to a batch of texts in the Bible that seems to suggest the Christian life is indeed a happy life. Peter makes it sound, in fact, like the Christian life is the most enviable sort of

---

word quite like our word "happiness" (which seems to be a much younger word, of much later derivation). "Joy" in the biblical sense is a complex emotional term, which doesn't admit of a simple definition but seems certainly to indicate a certain brightness of disposition and a certain smiling demeanor. Therefore, rather than concluding that "happiness" is a shallow worldly concept and "joy" is a deeper Christian concept, I think it better to conclude that "joy" in the biblical sense encompasses "happiness" in the contemporary sense. *In other words, "joy" is happiness and then some.* For our purposes here, I am using happiness, joy, contentment, satisfaction, etc., as synonymous. Understand then that by "happiness" I don't merely mean a superficial emotional state but rather a sense of genuine fulfillment, a genuine sense of contented joy. Frankly, I have chosen to use the word "happiness" rather than "joy" in most instances, because it holds more cultural sway with us. Because we are worldly Christians, generally speaking, we care about happiness deeply, but joy we could mostly do without.

life imaginable:

> *Though you have not seen him, you love him. Though you do not now see him, you believe in him and* ***rejoice with joy that is inexpressible and filled with glory****, obtaining the outcome of your faith, the salvation of your souls. (1 Pet 1.8-9 emphasis added)*

It's hard to imagine there are idols that can offer "joy that is inexpressible and filled with glory"! Maybe Peter is talking about a future heaven? No, look closely; this is not future bliss but present bliss. Though you do not "now" see Jesus, you rejoice with joy now—with happiness so wonderful it defies explanation with words. The psalmist seems to concur with Peter:

> *I have set the Lord always before me; because he is at my right hand, I shall not be shaken. Therefore* ***my heart is glad, and my whole being rejoices****; my flesh also dwells secure...You make known to me the path of life; in your presence there is* ***fullness of joy; at your right hand are pleasures forevermore****. (Ps 16.8-11 emphasis added)*

The psalmist's whole being rejoiced (i.e., was full of joy), as he knew a fullness of happiness in this life, while also looking forward to eternal pleasures in the age to come. Again, the context will not allow this to be speaking only of the future. With the Lord centrally before his eyes, he was filled to the brim with happiness. Consider another:

> *The kingdom of heaven is like treasure hidden in a field, which a man found and covered up. Then in his joy he goes and sells all that he has and buys that field. (Mt 13.44)*

The man finds in the field something he values so highly above everything else that "in his joy" he sells all he has. His excitement is frantic and hasty. All his belongings, all his earthly joys are valueless in light of the value he finds in the field. Is it the unhappy life he finds in the field? You wouldn't think so. The man's decision seems easy, and he does not second guess it. He sees nothing in the world worth holding onto except the field.

Let's look at one more. Paul at times seems so happy, he can barely decide whether he wants to go on living or to die and be with Jesus:

> *...Christ is proclaimed, and in that I rejoice. Yes, and I will rejoice, for I know that through your prayers and the help of the Spirit of Jesus Christ this will turn out for my deliverance, as it is my eager expectation and hope that I will not be at all ashamed, but that with full courage now as always Christ will be honored in my body, whether by life or by death. For to me to live is Christ, and to die is gain. If I am to live in the flesh, that means fruitful labor for me. Yet which I shall choose I cannot tell. I am hard pressed between the two. My desire is to depart and be with Christ, for that is far better. But to remain in the flesh is more necessary on your account. Convinced of this, I know that I will remain and continue with you all, for your progress and joy in the faith, so that in me you may have ample cause to glory in Christ Jesus, because of my coming to you again. (Phil 1.18b-26)*

Paul is full of joy, rejoicing (v 18). He plans on rejoicing more in the near future (v 18b). He wants to visit the Philippians again soon for their "progress and joy in the faith" (v 25) so they may "glory in Christ Jesus" (v 26). I should think Paul is here on a luxury vacation, sending a postcard regarding all the sights and sounds he is seeing, all the delights and delicacies, but where is he? He is in chains, in prison (cf. 1.13). Sometimes I think even the best among us in this age are merely lukewarm Christians, all missing out on true life.

We have to back up though. Isn't this suggestion–that the Christian life is the happiest life for man–contradicted by other elements in the Bible? The Bible talks certainly of duty and sacrifice, does it not? Should we ignore the 1000 verses that talk about duty and sacrifice in favor of the 100 that speak as if the Christian life were man's happiest life after all? For instance, I have mentioned this passage several times:

> *Then Jesus told his disciples, "If anyone would come after me, let him deny himself and take up his cross and follow me. For whoever would save his life will lose it, but whoever loses his life for my sake will find it. For what will it profit a man if he gains the whole world and forfeits his soul? "(Mt 16.24-26)*

We sometimes interpret this to mean that, in order to follow Jesus, we must give up our temporal happiness, but is that the real meaning? Is Jesus really saying "give up your life on earth to go to heaven"? That doesn't seem quite right. Isn't a far more plausible interpretation "let him deny [his worldly, deceitful desires] and take up his cross and follow me. For whoever would save his life [for worldly, deceitful desires] will lose it, but whoever loses his life [of worldly, deceitful desires] for my sake will find it"? Read it again and again and again and again. He promises that in him we will find *life*. In promising us life, is he promising us the best life possible on earth, or is he merely promising an unhappy life with a last-minute happy ending?

Logically, saying "whoever saves his life will lose [his life]" and "whoever loses his life will find [his life]" is nonsense, contradictory, unless Jesus is using the word "life" in two different ways. This is clearly what he was doing. While the inclination of our hearts is to search for life in our stupid, half-baked hobbies or interests—in worldly things, as if to try to gain the whole world—Jesus would have us find life instead in him. He does not say to give up your life on earth to go to heaven, as we so poorly read him at times. Rather, he says to give up the life of worldliness, which is not really life, and instead find that life which is real, satisfying, and joyous. Give up the life of being enslaved to things that don't care about you to gain life in service to the God who loves you and seeks your true good, your true happiness, your true and lasting pleasure. We might paraphrase Jesus, "Whoever denies his old, false self and loses his so-called 'life' for my sake will find real life." Jesus came that we might have life, and have it to the full (Jn 10.10 NIV).

But the Bible surely talks about duty and sacrifice? Look closely at the principle Paul lays out in 2 Corinthians:

> *The point is this: whoever sows sparingly will also reap sparingly, and whoever sows bountifully will also reap bountifully. Each one must give as he has decided in his heart, not reluctantly or under compulsion, for God loves a cheerful giver. And God is able to make all grace abound to you, so that having all sufficiency in all things at all times, you may abound in every good work. As it is written,*
>
> *"He has distributed freely, he has given to the poor;*
> *his righteousness endures forever."*
>
> *He who supplies seed to the sower and bread for food will supply and multiply your seed for sowing and increase the harvest of your righteousness. You will be enriched in every way to be generous in every way, which through us will produce thanksgiving to God. For the ministry of this service is not only supplying the needs of the saints but is also overflowing in many thanksgivings to God. (2 Cor 9.6-12)*

Is giving to the needy and to the church a duty? Of course. Is giving your money away a sacrifice? Obviously, yes, everyone likes money. The point is not that there is no such thing as duty or sacrifice; the point is that Christian duty is precisely where Christians find their delight. If we are to give, we are to give cheerfully with thanksgiving. Sow sparingly as a Christian, expect to reap sparingly. Give bountifully and you will reap bountifully, and you will be "enriched in every way," "having all sufficiency in all things at all times." God loves one who does his duty with joy. The one who works "reluctantly" or "under compulsion" is missing the whole point and losing much of his reward. Working without joy sucks all the worth right out of it. Our "ministry" and "service," according to Paul, is "overflowing in many thanksgivings to God." Strangely enough, if we're doing it right, pleasing God is precisely the thing that pleases us.

If you have followed the plot thus far, you know we have already learned that, while sin promises the world, in the end it just takes and takes and never satisfies. It never lives up to its promises. What is true of the part is true of the whole; it is dissatisfying every single time, and the sum of all sin is still just empty dissatisfaction. The first time didn't end well, and the last time won't end well. Sin starts out small but balloons over time and eventually consumes the whole field of vision. It hangs the carrot in front of your nose as bait and promises deep satisfaction. So you start to chase it down the wide road, but you never end up arriving at your destination. Sin begins to affect every other aspect of your life, inviting you ever deeper into a course of anger, bitterness, and ungratefulness. You work hard, anticipate much, but reap little.

> *Now, therefore, thus says the Lord of hosts: Consider your ways. You have sown much, and harvested little. You eat, but you never have enough; you drink, but you never have your fill. You clothe yourselves, but no one is warm. And he who earns wages does so to put them into a bag with holes. (Hag 1.6)*

Sin promises life but tends always toward death. When you look for satisfaction—for happiness—in sin, you never find it. In fact, the Bible teaches that God actively makes unrighteous people unhappy so they will turn away from their sin and turn instead to him:

> *The Lord knows how to rescue the godly from trials,* ***and to keep the unrighteous under punishment until the day of judgment****, and especially those who indulge in the lust of defiling passion and despise authority. (2 Pet 2.9-10 emphasis added)*

Look closely at the immediate context before and after. This is not talking about the unrighteous who have already died; it's talking about the unrighteous who are very much alive. If the unrighteous could find true contentment, they would never perceive their need for God, but God is actively involved in their unhappiness, as if the divine finger were always weighing down on them, preventing them from ever finding real contentment in sin. Their life is one of punishment; God punishes them so they may turn to the true joy of knowing Jesus. Their conscience alternates constantly between accusing and excusing themselves. They build elaborate philosophical systems to convince themselves that God will not condemn them in the end, but still their misery and worry persists to the end. They may say they are perfectly content, but this is merely a combination of deceit and self-deception. So, then, can we conclude that the Bible teaches that the life of sin is man's happiest temporal choice? No, we can't. It teaches precisely the opposite: that the Christian life is the renewal of true joy—joy as it was originally intended—joy as joy should be.

Think of the cosmic injustice there would be if sinful pursuits could satisfy man more than walking with Jesus! Could it really be that God wants his followers on earth with their heads hung low, detesting their lives, with but the faintest glimmer of hope for a better turn of events in the next life to keep them from keeling over on the spot? Could it be that the all-knowing God did not think through human psychology enough to know that people who joyously loved him—happily loved him—would make better worshipers? Better soldiers in his spiritual warfare (Eph 6.10-18)? Better brothers and sisters to his Only-begotten (1 Jn 3.1-3)? Has he not heard that you get more flies with honey than vinegar? Could Jesus expect anyone to want to follow his followers if they were the most unhappy sort of people?

Could it be that the most important commandment of all is to love the Lord with all of ourselves, with every single thing in ourselves (Mt 22.34-40) and that somehow our happiness in doing so is excluded from the list and is of no importance to God? If a girl were to say, "I love my boyfriend," we would take it to mean that she delights in him, that she values him, that she is committed to him, that she is satisfied by him, that she cannot help but to talk about him and shower him with gifts. Could it be then, in contrast to this, that when God commands love he only means duty and a submissive, begrudging obedience? Does he not also want our genuine affection? To love something is to enjoy that thing, to be satisfied by that thing. The judgment of Martyn Lloyd-Jones is accurate beyond question when he concludes that "you cannot read through your New Testament without seeing at a glance that joy is meant to be an essential part of the Christian experience."[56]

Consider this: What father, when he asks his children to do something, enjoys when they throw a fit, and then when they are compelled by threats finally to obey, they do it begrudgingly, detesting the one who gave the commandment and spoiled their fun? I don't want my boys to love me out of duty, because they are compelled to. That would be an insult to any father. I want them to love me and obey me because I am a good father,[57] because they know I have their best interest in mind, and because they delight in me. I want them to *want* to love and obey me. I want them to find great happiness in loving me, just as I find great happiness in loving them. They don't have to choose between loving me and being happy themselves. I hope they find their happiness precisely in loving me and obeying my commandments, which are intended for their good, to set them on the joyous path of self-discipline and integrity.

I think sometimes we are taught that God's rewards are all reserved for heaven and that it is selfish to think too much about rewards, even though Jesus commanded us to seek treasures in heaven![58] We are subtly taught that the concern for our own happiness is a selfish and misdirected concern, as if we could just turn it off with the flip of a switch. The Christian life, we are told, is the life of duty, of obligation, of sacrifice, of forgoing one's true delight (in sin, although not polite to say it

56 D. Martyn Lloyd-Jones, *Spiritual Depression: It's Causes and Cure* (Grand Rapids, MI: Wm. B. Eerdmans, 1965), 110.

57 I'm trying much harder now, anyway!

58 cf. Matthew 6.20

that way) and instead opting to humbly and unfortunately take up your cross and follow him. To some degree, I used to believe God delighted in my service only if I *didn't* delight in it. This thought expressed itself in numerous ways. I often thought that the more you disliked something but did it anyway, just to prove how great your love was for God, the greater the reward would be. I remember being proud of myself at times for taking so little delight in things that I did out of duty, as if God valued the somber giver more than he valued the cheerful giver. I even remember trying not to enjoy things for fear my joy in it would somehow ruin the goodness of it, as if the only way to be a proper Christian was to hate every moment of it.

In the wake of my repentance, as time elapsed and I began to see things more clearly, I began to allow for the possibility that perhaps I had, my whole life, been looking at everything backwards, the way zombies are always inclined to. Perhaps in my mind, I was making evil good and good evil. Perhaps the forbidden fruit was not the path to wisdom and happiness after all.

Even though forbidden fruit sounds delicious and obedience sounds dreadful, will the fruit really make me happier today than obedience? No one can deny that fruit sounds better than obedience. Everyone loves fruit, and everyone hates obedience! Wretched obedience and glorious fruit! Only a liar can deny that the forbidden fruit sounds full of wonders and wonderful, with wisdom as its pit and core. Only a dishonest person can deny that the concept of obedience stinks in our nostrils of death! Everybody hates obedience! The sound of it is like nails on a chalkboard. Wretched obedience and glorious fruit! But friends, is this reality or is it merely false perception? Is it Truth, or is it deceitful desires playing tricks on us? If you are a Christian, I suspect you know the answer. Oh friends, weep and mourn, we are in deep, very deep. We are in up to our eyeballs and then some. We are in need of saving, and we cannot do it on our own.

God had to shake me fiercely to get me to see there was something desperately wrong with the way I secretly believed the life of sin was man's happiest option and the way I secretly believed the Christian life was a dreary and unhappy sort of life. I had perpetually fostered a worldly outlook that saw its greatest good in sin, and so only begrudgingly followed God out of a servile sense of obligation and guilt. I followed God only insofar as it seemed to be sufficient enough to keep me out of hell. This worldly mindset everywhere masquerades as Christianity, but Christianity it is not.

Maybe you're suspicious. Maybe this whole line of reasoning sounds a bit selfish. But consider for a moment that selfishness is not as simple as we make it out to be. Certainly self-interest is wicked when the object of our self-interest is world worship, yes. Certainly we would say that, when Adam ate of the fruit of the tree, he was being selfish. He did not care at all about the endless misery he was bringing upon us all. If he made it to heaven,[59] we shall each have to take a turn punching him in the gut. But think for a moment: What if Adam had not eaten of the fruit and had followed the path of obedience, wanting to prove his faithfulness, wanting to grow even closer to God, to be rewarded with more of God and commended by God for his faithful service? What if he intelligently recognized that the fruit could not satisfy him, but only God could satisfy him, and he thirsted for more of God and for more personal satisfaction in God? Would we still call it selfishness? What if we are "selfish" for righteousness? What if we are greedy to be holy? Worldly self-interest leads to death; yes, it fragments all society, but godly self-interest is the path to life and healing. As one Puritan wrote:

> *Oh, covet more grace. Never think you have enough. It is good and honest avarice. We are [commanded] to covet the best things (1 Corinthians 12:31). It is a heavenly ambition when we desire to be high in God's favor, a blessed contention when all the strife is over who shall be the most holy.*[60]

59 Which is not entirely clear.

60 Thomas Watson, *The Art of Divine Contentment* (Grand Rapids, MI: Soli Deo

Coveting is a sin when the aim is worldly gain. Trying to selfishly outdo everyone else is death when the object in view is evil. But listen to Paul:

> *Love one another with brotherly affection. Outdo one another in showing honor. (Rom 12.10)*

There is no law at all against desiring good, spiritual things (Gal 5.23). Get all you can get of righteousness and the satisfaction and peace that comes with it. Strive vigorously to be satisfied with the joy of knowing Jesus Christ! The search to be happy is normal and good. God made it, and there is nothing at all wrong with it. Among men, self-love is a given. Everyone wants to be satisfied, and everyone is concerned for themselves. "For no one ever hated his own flesh, but nourishes and cherishes it" (Eph 5.29). Nobody can turn off his interest in his own well-being. The monk who lights himself on fire still does so because he thinks there is something to be gained by doing it, if only in the next life. When self-love terminates upon sin, when sin is the end goal, self-interest leads to death. But when we come to recognize our true joy is not found in sin but in righteousness, we find service to God and service to others is also service to self. The Christian is like Christ in that our greatest good is found, strangely enough, in sacrifice. Jesus said the least will be the greatest, and I think part of what he meant is that the one who gives the most will himself have the most, both in this life and the next.[61]

God's plan is seamless and works out well for everyone who loves him. It's not a matter of turning off your interest in your own happiness, but rather turning it up, and redirecting and refocusing it away from sin and unto God. Satan, however, tries to make things feel disjointed. He tries to create a rift between us and God. He does his best to disincentivize

---

Gloria Publications, 2011), 103.

61 cf. Luke 18:29-30, where Jesus specifically said the Christian life offers many rewards in this life.

us, just as he did with Adam and Eve. He creates a false dilemma and tries to persuade us that we must choose either to be happy ourselves or to worship God. But what if we find our greatest satisfaction in worship? What if the thing God designed us for–to worship him–is the very same thing that inevitably brings us the most pleasure? That would be a clever design, would it not? What if God is most satisfied with us at the same time that we are most satisfied with him? The truth is, there is no conflict in the Bible between love of God, love of others, and love of self. It's not as though you have to choose only one of them; you can have all three. Christian service, in love, is giving to others, giving to God, but also yourself growing closer to God, which naturally yields a great harvest of personal satisfaction, both now and forever.

Now in some ways Christian happiness is mysterious. When a person is spiritually dead or spiritually cold and they hear about Jesus dying on the cross for sin, it sounds to them like a distant fairy tale. Perhaps the slightest particle of a tear creeps to the corner of their eye at the thought of the selflessness of the act, but in the end they are unmoved, and their sinful habits remain unchanged. This may be even worse in a person who is well-versed in Christian doctrine but has grown cold in his faith, who feels he knows all there is to know about the matter, and who may even justify his lack of enthusiasm by the fact that he is not being fed constantly with new truths like the zealous new believer.

Contrast this with those whose hearts are warm because they have been daily diligent and have been fighting the cold and darkness off with sword and shield. They can hear that story over and over and weep and be renewed each time, feeling anew the great weight of sin lifted from their shoulders. I have to think that in heaven, when a billion years have passed and when the saints have heard that story a billion times, they will still, as the true children of God, be on their edge of their beds bugging their Father to tell that story—the one about how God turned horror into eternal bliss—just one more time. Never be misled into thinking there's something wrong with the Bible or that there's something wrong with all of the churches in your town. The Bible is sufficient for the least and the greatest, and even the best of preachers preaches also to those who, though hearing, do not hear (Mt 13.13). There is nothing wrong with my Bible, there is nothing wrong with my church, but there is something desperately wrong with *me*!

What hope do we have in succeeding at the Christian life unless we genuinely believe there is more joy to be found in the things of God than in sin? Maybe we can do it for a week or a month, perhaps even for a whole year, but can we really go a lifetime on the unhappy narrow path of righteousness, all the while seeing all the fun there is to be had on the wide road nearby, that roller coaster with no waiting in line? Look around you; look once more. Look again at our waistlines and how we spend our time. Are we the type of people who are willing to defer immediate pleasure for long-term gain? Isn't it much more likely that we'll just be swept along with the crowd of zombies on the wide road, if we consciously believe the truly happy life is to be found *over there*? We simply have no hope of succeeding as Christians unless we become genuinely convinced that choosing Christ is the happy choice, the pleasurable choice, in every instance. We must no longer mope and trudge along in duty, but rather run with the conviction that in Christ is life to the full! We must rid ourselves of every little lie that tries to convince us sin is our better option *in any respect whatsoever*! We must root out the lie in every corner and force the lie into submission to Christ (2 Cor 10.5). If God is anything, God is righteous, and in God's world, there can't be a meaningful downside to righteousness. When the world is finally rid of unrighteousness, we shall call it heaven, and heaven it will be.

With a singularity of purpose, for decades now, John Piper, the contemporary pastor and writer, has sought to convince us that the Christian life—the life of wholeheartedly seeking after the face of God—is a satisfying and joyous life. It is a message we need to seriously evaluate if we are to have hope of making any progress as Christians and a message our culture desperately needs if Christianity is to offer any appeal. Piper's central theme runs through all of his thought and writings: *God is most glorified in us, when we are most satisfied in him.* I refer you to him for more insights on this subject and answers to further objections that may present themselves.[62] You could also do worse than to check out my book on the Christian Hedonism, which is a more thorough and systematic defense of many of these ideas.[63] If you find this hard to stomach for one reason or another, at least consider the possibility that you have been duped. You owe it to yourself to investigate further and to make a deeper inquiry than I can offer in this short space.

We must pause now for a couple of warnings. The Christian life is the happiest life for man, but that is not to deny that we will all have hardships. That is not to say Christianity guarantees a life without stress or struggle. It surely does not. In fact, the Christian life guarantees that you will constantly have to battle your own flesh, the devil, and the world (Eph 2.2-3). I am not saying the Christian life is a life without suffering; I am simply saying the Christian life, the life of diligently seeking after God through Christ, is the only life that offers the possibility of true and genuine happiness and contentment, both in this life and the next.

Nor should we think the Christian life will ever be all happiness without any grief. Think of the culmination of the Bible in the death of Christ. Our greatest moment of weeping is at the same time our greatest moment of joy. They killed the gentle Lamb! But his blood washed away our sins! This is true of the whole Christian experience. The life of Jesus was, on the one hand, a paradise of closeness with his Father and, on the other, a serious and somber march toward certain death. He was led like a lamb to the slaughter (Isa 53.7). No one took his life from him; he laid down his life of his own consent (Jn 10.18). The truth is that, as Christian happiness increases, so too Christian discontent increases. "A

62 www.desiringgod.org. Also see the bibliography at the end of the book.

63 The Secret of Sacrificial Self-Service: Discovering the Spiritual Incentives of Christian Hedonism. This book was also written subsequent to the current work, as publishing woes led to several delays with the present work.

true Christian is a wonder. He is the most content, yet the least satisfied."[64] As I grow closer to God, my sense of sin becomes more acute, and I am more dissatisfied with that aspect of myself. As my happiness in Christ increases, so too my dissatisfaction increases at how the world chooses to actively discredit and disregard his obvious and objective worth.

Christian sadness is not like the world's sadness, however. Our sadness never promotes despair in us but rather more fervent and vigorous action. Our sadness leads to more efficient warring with our sin and with the world. We are afflicted, but not crushed, perplexed, but not despairing, persecuted, but not forsaken, struck down, but not destroyed (2 Cor 4.8-9).

Happiness is an elusive thing. It's not like our thoughts, which we can direct here and there, wherever we want them to go. It is strangely outside of our control. We can't simply *will* ourselves to be happy. It can only be discovered indirectly. If you want to be happy, seek God's righteousness in the face of Christ, and happiness will come as a result. Seek the Kingdom of God first, and everything else that you need will come as a result of this (Mt 6.33), including happiness. If you seek happiness directly, it will always elude you. Instead, seek righteousness to discover happiness:

> If you want to be truly happy and blessed, if you would like to know true joy as a Christian, here is the prescription—'Blessed (truly happy) are they who do hunger and thirst after righteousness' [Mt 5.6]—not after happiness. Do not go on seeking thrills; seek righteousness. Turn to yourself, turn to your feelings and say: 'I have no time to worry about feelings, I am interested in something else. I want to be happy but still more I want to be righteous, I want to be holy. I want to be like my Lord, I want to live in this world as He lived, I want to

64 Thomas Watson, *The Art of Divine Contentment* (Grand Rapids, MI: Soli Deo Gloria Publications, 2011), 103.

> walk through it as He walked through it'...Set your whole aim upon righteousness and holiness and as certainly as you do so you will be blessed, you will be filled, you will get the happiness you long for. Seek for happiness and you will never find it, seek righteousness and you will discover you are happy—it will be there without your knowing it, without your seeking it. … If you find that your feelings are depressed do not sit down and commiserate with yourself, do not try to work something up but—this is the simple essence of it—go directly to Him and seek His Face.[65]

Nor should we expect that we can make a decision today to seek after God with our whole heart, decide to turn from the life of deceitful desires, and expect that tomorrow will be the happiest day of our life. We are, in fact, promised an intervening time of suffering. Before there is joy there is suffering and struggle, but the wait is not long:

Sing praises to the Lord, O you his saints,
and give thanks to his holy name.
For his anger is but for a moment,
and his favor is for a lifetime.
Weeping may tarry for the night,
but joy comes with the morning. (Ps 30.4-5)

Therefore, humble yourself, weep aloud and cry out to him, begin to walk rightly, wait patiently, and in time he will lift you up out of this swamp of despair.

I waited patiently for the Lord;
he inclined to me and heard my cry.
He drew me up from the pit of destruction,

65 D. Martyn Lloyd-Jones, *Spiritual Depression: It's Causes and Cure* (Grand Rapids, MI: Wm. B. Eerdmans, 1965), 117.

out of the miry bog,
and set my feet upon a rock,
making my steps secure.
He put a new song in my mouth,
a song of praise to our God. (Ps 40.1-3)

11

OUR GREATEST HAPPINESS IN "THINGS"

Behold the fat guy! Feast your eyes upon him and consider his ways.

Now I can't think I'll meet with any objections if I say, first of all, that food is good. Food is good in the objective sense, in that God made it. Food is good in the subjective sense, in that it tastes good and is enjoyable. Food is good in the utilitarian sense, in that it is functional—we need it to survive. Food is good in the spiritual sense, in that it teaches us spiritual lessons—the fruit of the Spirit, the bread of life, etc.—as well as in the ultimate sense, in that through the use of food God accomplishes all of his purposes on earth. Food is good; who can deny it?

I remember, when my great grandmother was well into her 90s, every time she would talk to my mom on the phone she would describe what she had for lunch and dinner that day. We used to laugh because it seemed like a trivial conversation piece, but we knew she talked about food because it was one of her few remaining joys. She lived by herself. Her mobility was somewhat limited. She didn't drive. She didn't watch TV. She only had one or two visitors each week, each only for an hour or two, so most of the time it was just her, her favorite chair, and her Bible, but she looked forward to each meal, and, as I reflect upon it now, she was a very happy lady. All of that is simply to say that food is a wonderful gift, an enjoyable experience, something to look forward to three times each day (four if you live near a Taco Bell).

Now, allowing that food is enjoyable and allowing that the obese person, generally speaking, eats more food, it must follow that the obese person has more enjoyment in food. Is this argument true or false? While it might be tempting to agree at first, given the persuasive form of the argument, no doubt a few minutes of reflection would yield the conclusion that the statement is false. On the subject of overeating, I can assure you I have a measure of expertise. The obese person approaches a meal usually with a bit of anxiety. We are anxious about being looked at while eating, anxious about not getting enough to eat, anxious that we will overeat and the cycle will continue. Because we are self-conscious, we often try to act modestly when offered food, as if it is our usual habit to abstain from food altogether, as if we "never touch the stuff." Then we sneak away from the crowd and gorge ourselves in secret. There are patterns of deception and concealment as with all sin. While eating, we continue to be anxious about not getting enough to eat, thinking about what we will eat next, and so forth, to such a degree that when we are finished eating we barely remember eating at all. The meal seemed like a vanishing illusion; the joy of it was stolen by fear and anxiety. We spent every bite thinking about the next bite rather than enjoying the present one. The food is gone; all that remains is the guilt, the self-loathing, and a certain bloated, unhealthy feeling.

All of us who carry around the proverbial "keg" instead of a "six-pack" know that, once we have fallen into a cycle of bad eating habits, it's very difficult to get out.[66] Food becomes a daily battle instead of the constant joy it was intended to be. At the farthest extremes, eating disorders represent the most obvious manifestations of this problem. No

66 It may be worth noting that the pursuit of six-packs can be an idol as well. As we have seen, the terrain is treacherous.

doubt a few have medical conditions that make it difficult to lose weight and keep it off. But for the rest of us, the vast majority of us, the fact is simply that we made a long series of bad decisions, most of them subtle. We feasted too often and fasted too little (probably never). We failed to be thankful for our food. We delighted in it as an end in itself rather than something designed to make us grateful to God. We ate regardless of hunger and other internal signals; we ate just for the sake of eating. We ate to console ourselves and to reward ourselves. We sought happiness in food, in and of itself, and before we knew it, the food we used to control took control over us. We used it for ends for which it was not intended and in ways in which it was not intended, and before we knew it we were trapped in a cycle of sin. The food that God intended to be a blessing to us became a curse, because as the sinful use of food increased, the natural pleasure in food decreased at a roughly proportionate rate. This is surely as close as we're likely to get to Christ's teaching that "everyone who practices sin is a slave to sin" (Jn 8.34, also Rom 6).

As with all other earthly things, food was intended to serve the purpose of making us grateful, of drawing us closer to God, and to the degree that it does not accomplish that, it is sin. Whether we eat or drink, all is to be for the glory of God. Anything less is a moral failure at some level. If you are a gamer, your gaming must be for God's glory. If you are a Facebooker, your Facebooking must be for God's glory. Whatever it is is that you are, you must seek the glory of God before all else. This should give us a sense of how heavy our sin really is when held up to God's righteous standard. Have I ever eaten a single meal without a little bit of sin in it, a sin which, at the same time, stole my joy from me? How horrible is the weight of our sin in this case! Perhaps like the mess left behind by the Cat in the Hat (one of my kids' favorites), "this mess is so big and so deep and so tall, we can not pick it up. There is no way at all!"[67] And yet how wonderful to have a Savior to cast this weight upon!

---

67 Dr. Seuss, *The Cat in the Hat* (New York, NY: Random House, 1957), 55.

> *For I delight in the law of God, in my inner being, but I see in my members another law waging war against the law of my mind and making me captive to the law of sin that dwells in my members. Wretched man that I am! Who will deliver me from this body of death? Thanks be to God through Jesus Christ our Lord! (Rom 7.22-25)*

A war rages inside of us, but in Christ we are already victors. In Christ, we are legally blameless before God, righteous children, always improving at acting like free children rather than slaves to sin. We find great "delight in the law of God" (v 22) since it no longer binds us as a taskmaster, and since we know that God's law is the path to true joy. When we see the Son of God face to face, the battle will be over. When we see him, we will instantly be like him (1 Jn 3.2). The seed of life planted in us at our conversion or rebirth, which grows steadily into maturity through a lifetime of faith, will then be instantly full grown.

Let us backtrack then. Food is most enjoyable when used appropriately. Generally speaking, the fit person is not so self-conscious when he eats; he enjoys his food more naturally; he has good habits; he plans ahead and brings enough to ensure fullness, but not so much that he will feel sick afterward. There is, therefore, no ensuing guilt after a meal. Going even further, the fit Christian person—healthy both in body and spirit—is able to surpass this still. He has no guilt but all the joy, all the pleasure, and along with this he praises God for his meal. He sees in each bite a God who loves his pleasure. He recognizes God as the author of every distinctive flavor, and he marvels at the breadth of God's imagination and creativity. He makes a habit of gratitude. His belly is full and his heart is full of adoration; his meal becomes a moment of worship, an instrument in the service of God. Burroughs is spot-on:

> *If there is any good in wealth or in any comfort in this world, it is not so much that it pleases my senses or that it suits my body, but that it has reference to God, the first being, that by these*

> *[created things] somewhat of God's goodness might be conveyed to me, and I may have a sanctified use of the creature [i.e. created thing] to draw me nearer to God, and be made more serviceable for his glory in the place where he has set me: this is the good of the creature.*[68]

Your hobbies and interests should all lead to gratitude to the God who gave them to you. You should thank God for them and use them as a means of growing closer to him. They should never be ends in themselves. All satisfaction should tend unto worship:

> *For everything created by God is good, and nothing is to be rejected if it is received with thanksgiving, for it is made holy by the word of God and prayer. (I Tim 4.4-5)*

The teaching of Paul here seems to be that "every-thing" should be used to make us a "thanks-giving" type of people. Every *thing* should be unto the joy of worship. Every detail of our lives is to be sanctified through prayer and thanksgiving. The world is not bad; the world is good. God "richly provides us with everything to enjoy" (1 Tim 6.17). Our sin is not that we use the things in the world; our sin is that we use things foolishly, as ends in themselves, without regard to God at all. We worship the *things* themselves rather than worshipping God through them. But the only way to truly delight in the things in the world is to use them to grow closer to God. Here is the principle I am after: *We take the most pleasure in things when things are used appropriately, which is to say, used to direct us to God.* To summarize what we have said so far, *Man's greatest happiness is found in the worship of God and not in the worship of things. Likewise, man finds his greatest delight in things when he uses them as a means of worshiping God.* Man's chief end, that is, the meaning of life according to the Christian belief system, is to glorify God and

---

68 Jeremiah Burroughs, *The Rare Jewel of Christian Contentment* (1648; repr., Carlisle, PA: The Banner of Truth Trust, 2009), 91.

to enjoy him forever.[69]

Here is my overall argument: *A life centered upon God, the life of worship, with things in their appropriate places means not only the happiest future life possible, but also the happiest temporal life possible, and also the most happiness possible in earthly things.*

The Christian life is our happiest possible option, both now and in the hereafter. Do you believe it? If not, keep searching, keep questioning, keep reading; be fully convinced there is no truth taught herein. You owe it to yourself to investigate further. If you do believe it, has there ever been an easier decision? I have rejoiced—wept with joy—many times in these months, having discovered that God has made our decision so easy. Jesus doesn't want to crush our joy; Jesus wants us to have life, and to have it more abundantly (Jn 10.10 KJV). Jesus doesn't ask us to forgo our pleasure; he asks us to re-evaluate the true source of pleasure and to have more pleasure in the pursuits of his kingdom. Jesus doesn't ask us to stop doing *things*; rather, he asks us to do them appropriately, which is also how they are best savored. Working hard and earning something is enjoyable; when you steal a thing, that thing seems to come with a mountain of emotional baggage. People who steal things never appreciate them or take good care of them; instead they see them as disposable and valueless. Similarly, sex inside of marriage is meant for our guilt-free satisfaction, but outside of marriage it never seems to go right; it ends in hurt feelings and resentment at one end of the spectrum and mass genocide in the form of convenient, clinical abortions at the other end. Worldly things bring us the most happiness when used appropriately, that is, in the service of God, in the spirit of wholehearted worship, in conformity with God's teachings in the Bible.

Don't misunderstand me, and don't let your sin mislead you. I'm certainly not encouraging you to become a Christian (or a better Christian) only to maximize your fun in your worldly endeavors. That

69 Westminster Shorter Catechism, question 1.

still makes sin central in your thinking and is, therefore, a form of hypocrisy. What I'm saying is that if you pursue righteousness above all else, then your worldly interests will fall back into their proper place and you will enjoy them as they were intended, for the end for which they were intended, that is, for the God who intends everything for your good (Rom 8.28). Only when you enjoy everything in Christ do you enjoy anything to the full. Worldly pursuits become moments of sanctified worship, as if they too were washed in the precious blood of Jesus.

We sometimes think of God as a divine killjoy, who hates our happiness because he's always prohibiting us from having fun with our sin, but the opposite is true—at the same time that sin steals God's worship from Him, so too it steals our happiness from us. Ask yourself this simple question: how much do you *stress* over your hobbies? This is the simple litmus test: you know you are a *slave* to them when they are a *stress* to you. Anxiety over your hobbies is a sure sign of spiritual addiction and world worship, a sure sign that you have come to esteem them higher than they ought to be esteemed, and that as a result they have become a taskmaster over you.

Likewise, if sin can convince us the life of sin is the life of real happiness, we have already lost the battle, we are already enslaved. If, on the other hand, we are fully convinced in our minds (even if our hearts lag behind) that at every moment and in every instance the choice of righteousness will bring us more happiness than the choice for sin, we have made a great step in Christian sanctification. Sin will have a much harder time overcoming those who are convinced that the life of sin is an unhappy life for man, despite first appearances.

Jesus knows that we have managed to get everything backwards, to become enslaved and burdened by the demands of our own interests. He knows that we desperately need freedom and rest. He is able to set us free from slavery (Jn 8.32), free indeed (8.36):

At that time Jesus declared, "I thank you, Father, Lord of heaven and earth, that you have hidden these things from the wise and understanding and revealed them to little children; yes, Father, for such was your gracious will... Come to me, all who labor and are heavy laden, and I will give you rest. Take my yoke upon you, and learn from me, for I am gentle and lowly in heart, and you will find rest for your souls. For my yoke is easy, and my burden is light." (Mt 11.25-30)

12

ONE FINAL MOTIVATION

Hopefully we have found a couple of great motivations for putting worldly interests in their proper place and for making our relationship with God our central focus. We have investigated God's offer of temporal happiness, and we have discovered the greatest potential of happiness in worldly things. Richard Winter summarizes our alternatives well:

> *Ultimately, we are faced with a choice. We can choose to surf the channels, the Web or the waves in order to try to satisfy our desire for "something more," our craving for the next exciting fix to make us feel alive and to relieve our boredom. Or we can choose to respond to the call to love and serve the true and living God who promises to satisfy our pangs of hunger and to quench our deepest thirst for meaning and significance.*[70]

Perhaps you remain unconvinced. Perhaps your mom gave you this book to straighten you out, and you just want to finish it so she will get off your back. I have a good mom too, who did the same sort of thing many times. Perhaps you feel content where you are, going to church enough to appease your conscience and to perhaps sneak in the

70 Richard Winter, *Still Bored in a Culture of Entertainment* (Downner Grove, IL: Intervarsity Press, 2002), 141-142.

back door of heaven. Going back a couple of years, I often told myself *my problem is that I'm too content being a lousy Christian.* It's hard to be motivated to change when things are cushy, quiet, and comfortable.

Here is a final thought, one last attempt at shaking you back to life: Christians live like Christians—with God central—where unbelievers live like unbelievers—with other things central. The truth is, if we love the world we do not love God (1 Jn 2.15). You cannot serve two masters; to love the one is to hate the other (Mt 6.24). Perhaps you raised your hand to accept the free gift of salvation, and then your life continued as it was prior to that point. Perhaps you haven't given it much thought since then. If your plan is to live with God as a footnote to your life, I submit for your consideration the distinct possibility that you were never a true Christian. Good trees produce good fruit; bad trees produce bad fruit.

> *You will recognize them by their fruits. Are grapes gathered from thornbushes, or figs from thistles? So, every healthy tree bears good fruit, but the diseased tree bears bad fruit. A healthy tree cannot bear bad fruit, nor can a diseased tree bear good fruit. Every tree that does not bear good fruit is cut down and thrown into the fire. Thus you will recognize them by their fruits. (Mt 7.16-20)*

Every good tree bears good fruit. Where there is no good fruit, it follows that there is no good tree. In other words, a Christian who doesn't live like a Christian is a Christian *by name only.* In truth, such a person is a hypocrite and an unbeliever. The apostle John is always crystal clear in his meaning. He explains to us how we can tell if we're really a Christian:

And by this we know that we have come to know him, if we keep his commandments. Whoever says "I know him" but does not keep his commandments is a liar, and the truth is not in him, but whoever keeps his word, in him truly the love of God is perfected. By this we may know that we are in him: whoever says he abides in him ought to walk in the same way in which he walked. (1 Jn 2.3-6)

Believing certain things to be true about God does not get you anything. You may genuinely believe the God of the Bible is real and Jesus died on the cross, but merely assenting to certain historical truths must not be confused with saving faith. Satan himself believes all of these things, but he is certainly no Christian:

> *You believe that God is one; you do well. Even the demons believe—and shudder! Do you want to be shown, you foolish person, that faith apart from works is useless? (Jas 2.19-20)*

Faith is an event, but it's an event that continues on forever. Genuine saving faith recognizes the awfulness of its own sin and feels the burden of its own guilt. When hearing the gospel, the faithful person rejoices to place this burden upon Christ and trusts in Christ alone, through faith alone, for salvation, that is, for the legal cleansing of his past, present, and future sins in the sight of God. True Christians know they cannot take away their own sin or purchase their way into heaven through their own deeds. Only faith in Jesus can take away sin. Redeemed man is, therefore, *legally* sinless before God, justified, reconciled, at peace with God forever, adopted as God's child. Christians love Jesus because of this gift. They long to see, understand, and to emulate their Savior. Genuine faith produces action. You cannot say, "I have faith that in ten seconds a meteor is going to fall on the spot on which I am standing right now," and yet not step to the side. Faith and works are organically connected. Faith and works automatically suppose one another. To believe something is to act upon your belief. To be faithful is to also be faithful in your actions. A person who is *unfaithful* in their actions is also unfaithful in principle. You cannot say to Jesus, "I believe everything you're saying here, but I'm not actually going to do any of it. My belief is not actually going to change the way I act." It's not faith; it's merely self-deception. Your sin has fooled you; your good deeds will not save you; your planning will fail you; hell awaits you. Do not be deceived. Jonathan Edwards

(1703-1758), considered by many to be America's most important philosophical theologian, describes the demise of world worshipers:

> *Your wickedness makes you as it were heavy as lead, and to tend downwards with great weight and pressure towards hell; and if God should let you go, you would immediately sink and swiftly descend and plunge into the bottomless gulf, and your healthy constitution, and your own care and prudence, and best contrivance, and all your righteousness, would have no more influence to uphold you and keep you out of hell, than a spider's web would have to stop a falling rock. Were it not for the sovereign pleasure of God, the earth would not bear you one moment; for you are a burden to it; the creation groans with you; the creature is made subject to the bondage of your corruption, not willingly; the sun does not willingly shine upon you to give you light to serve sin and Satan; the earth does not willingly yield her increase to satisfy your lusts; nor is it willingly a stage for your wickedness to be acted upon; the air does not willingly serve you for breath to maintain the flame of life in your vitals, while you spend your life in the service of God's enemies. God's creatures [i.e., created things] are good, and were made for men to serve God with, and do not willingly subserve to any other purpose, and groan when they are abused to purposes so directly contrary to their nature and end.* [71]

Don't sleep again until you have pounded on every pastor's door in the entire city and you find one who will explain to you the path of life. Don't sleep again until you can drift off knowing that your sins have been forever forgiven. True faith doesn't investigate tomorrow or the day after; it frantically searches right now. The gate is narrow and few enter it. If you believe that many, most, or all will make it in the narrow gate,

---

71 From his sermon, "Sinners in the Hands of an Angry God."

and that the narrow gate is, in fact, exceedingly wide, you are mistaken.

Along with those who are banking on having once raised their hand in a service, I suspect there exists another group among us. Perhaps you were, like me, passionate for a while, but your enjoyment in Christianity diminished, and your plan is to continue with God as peripheral. Beware of beginning something without finishing it.

> *Jesus said to him, "No one who puts his hand to the plow and looks back is fit for the kingdom of God." (Lk 9.62)*

Don't kid yourself into thinking you'll be fine to continue as you are. Self-deception is a frightening reality you cannot deny if you take the Bible with any seriousness.

The true Christian has two great sources of assurance as to the reality of his salvation and these two always point toward one another: faith and works. First, you must examine your faith. No one who sincerely hopes in Christ as Lord and Savior and recognizes their own inability to obey the law will be put to shame in the end, but it's up to you to examine yourself to make sure you have this sort of genuine faith. Paul assured us that "No one can say 'Jesus is Lord' except in the Holy Spirit" (1 Cor 12:3), and so if you can say "Jesus is Lord" and really mean it, then you can be confident that the Spirit dwells in you, and that you are Christ's and Christ is yours. Your sins are forgiven and it's all icing on the cake from here on out.

A further assurance of saving faith is the fruit that such a faith produces. "For faith is only real when there is obedience, never without it, and faith only becomes faith in the act of obedience."[72] Where faith is the cause and the fruit of good works is the necessary effect, you can be sure that without works there is no faith. Faith without works is dead, useless, ineffective, good for nothing (Jas 2.26). Your works testify

---

72 Bonhoeffer, Deitrich, *The Cost of Discipleship* (New York, New York: Touchstone, 1995), 64.

of your faith, and where the works are absent, the faith too is absent.

Don't kid yourself into thinking you can live a life characterized and dominated by sinful pursuits and yet still sneak into heaven in the end because you assented to certain historical facts. While taking my (ongoing) break from gaming, I remember thinking for the first month, "If God doesn't make me happy soon, I'll just go back to gaming as normal, since I was reasonably happy that way." It's a dark lie. It's sin looking back to the deceitful desires that it used to enjoy. It's sin making future provision for itself. Banish those thoughts; they'll destroy you in the end, and they'll plague you with misery until then. We think our time is our own and our bodies are our own and the things we own are our own, to do with them as we please, to waste and squander as we see fit—but therein lies our error. As the sole Creator of the cosmos, God owns the cosmos and everyone in it (cf. Ps 50.12). The Christian has been bought with a price (1 Cor 6.20). Make the best use of the time, because the days are evil (Eph 5.16). Remember, already "it is the last hour" (1 Jn 2.18).

The worship of God is mandatory, simply by our relationship to him as created beings. But our God is good, and because he seeks sincere and happy worship—worship in spirit and truth (Jn 4.23)[73]—he has made himself our greatest happiness. He does not make us choose between our happiness or his happiness, as we so often think, but rather, our happiness and his meet precisely in the moment of worship. He gets worship and we find our greatest happiness in the worship of him. Praise, thanksgiving, and gratefulness are pure acts of worship that open an endless spring of joy within our hearts. Pleasing him pleases us. He is most satisfied in us when we are most satisfied in him. He is not the simpleton we often make him out to be.

---

73 In "spirit" is to worship internally, with the heart, as opposed to merely going through the external, physical motions of worship. In "truth" is to worship God, as he presents himself in the Bible, in the way in which he dictates, as opposed to worshiping him as we would prefer him to be or in a manner in which we would prefer.

It is Satan who makes the world feel disjointed, who tries to convince us we have to choose between personal satisfaction or trying to satisfy God. He tries to convince us that it has to be one or the other, that we cannot have both, and that our desire for our own happiness is something selfish and evil. The old serpent sits laughing as he watches the Christian try to follow God begrudgingly, unwillingly, out of unhappy duty. Our sin tries to convince us it will bring us the most happiness where God is a joyless stick-in-the-mud. Sin would have us believe the author of joy, the source of all joy, knows nothing of joy at all. Sin tries its best to convince us that the all-knowing, all-present God is out of touch, a grey-bearded old bore in a rocking chair. Yet we know better; it simply cannot be that the author of all of these pleasures is not into pleasure. God is a hedonist at bottom; he has created this world for his own glory and satisfaction, and he invites us into his leisure and rest through the Bible and the finished work of the Son. The only reason we know what happiness is, is because God first knew happiness. His being is the very foundation of happiness. As he is love, so too he is happiness (cf. 1 Jn 4). The Father, Son, and Spirit are lacking in nothing; they find in themselves and their relationship to one another perfect love and perfect happiness and complete and unending joy. God could barely contain his infinite satisfaction, and so, in his vast wisdom, he conceived the perfect plan to adopt sons and daughters, to bring them into his intimate fellowship so they might partake of his perfect and complete joy along with him. He wants to share his joy with others; there is enough and more than enough for all who are willing to come. "You are all sons of God, through faith" (Gal 3.26). Through the Son we become sons! You have been adopted, as it were, into God's own family! Christ condescended to become man in order that he could ascend back to God with his redeemed brethren firmly in his grip. Kierkegaard writes:

> *There is so much said now about people being offended at Christianity because it is so dark and gloomy, offended at it*

> *because it is so severe, etc. It is now high time to explain that the real reason why man is offended at Christianity is because it is too high, because its goal is not man's goal, because it would make of a man something so extraordinary that he is unable to get it into his head.*[74]

This world cannot satisfy us, but the Son of God can. The learning curve of video games is limited, but the learning curve of knowing Jesus never ends. Through all eternal history there will be endless discovery for the one who walks with Jesus. Our greatest desire will be to know him better, and we shall each day drink our fill and be satisfied by his glory. We will be always hungry and always feasting on that bread of life, always thirsty and always drinking of that living water, and the better we did during our moment here in this life, the larger our appetite for his goodness will be. In God, there is an endless sea of pleasure and joy to be found, only limited by our individual capacity to take it all in. "Oh, taste and see that the Lord is good!" (Ps 34.8)

There is no need to put off this happy bliss until heaven. The process has already begun in the Christian:

> *The more of heaven that is in us, the less earth will content. When a person has once tasted the love of God, his thirst is much quenched toward earthly things. The joys of God's Spirit are heart-filling and heart-cheering joys. He who has these has heaven begun in him. (Romans 14:17)*[75]

As Christians, we "wander on earth and live in heaven."[76] Gather

---

74 Søren Kierkegaard, *The Sickness Unto Death* (Princeton, NJ: Princeton University Press, 1941), 94.

75 Thomas Watson, *The Art of Divine Contentment* (Grand Rapids, MI: Soli Deo Gloria Publications, 2011), 118.

76 Bonhoeffer, Deitrich, *The Cost of Discipleship* (New York, New York: Touchstone, 1995), 64.

a handful of promises to start on your journey; you'll find plenty more as you go. The way back leads to death; the way forward leads to that inexpressible and glory-filled joy, backed by the promises of Yahweh, the great I AM.

Do not be deceived into thinking the Christian way of life is optional for the Christian person; it is not. Christians live like Christians. Unbelievers live like unbelievers. If this upsets you, if this annoys you, it is because you are blinded by sin, a dead man walking, a self-deceived zombie. Do not be blind; turn, and live (Eze 18.32). If you must run unhappily at first, so be it, but do run. Your mourning will soon enough be turned to laughter.

13

FIGHTING FOR JOY

It's been six months since I've played video games. It's probably fairly obvious how I occupied most of that time. I pray often that the change and redirection in my life will remain permanent and that, whether I play again or not, I will carry with me always the clear vision that the Christian life, and not the life of sin, is life to the full. The free never again want to become unwilling slaves. "I have the right to do anything," says Paul, "but I will not be mastered by anything" (1 Cor 6.12).

Not being mastered by video games and technology, it seems to me, is only going to grow more difficult with the passage of time for our culture. Games are certainly not going away; they're only going to get better; they're going to have an ever-increasing appeal to an ever-broadening audience, and it won't be long before the last person who remembers a time before video games is dead and gone. Soon enough, it will no longer be considered the hobby of a few reclusive teenagers but will be a regular part of everyone's day. The natural trajectory of video games is obvious in its broad outline—each generation will find new ways to make them feel more real and less contrived.

The first generation of virtual reality products has arrived and seems to be here to stay. They are big and bulky and a far cry from Star Trek's "Holodeck," but will undoubtedly inch ever closer in that direction until the end of history. The educational possibilities and opportunities for evangelism will be limitless. On the other hand, it will be that much easier to live a life of sin without obvious physical consequences and that much easier to reach the Great Judgment only to discover that we missed the whole thing and that life passed us by while we allowed ourselves to be entertained into a numb, unending, and joyless stupor. How dreadful the thought of waking for the first time in the presence of God with nowhere to place your sin but upon yourself. How fearful to think the life of dissatisfaction in sin was the closest to heaven you ever got! May it not be so for any of us! This life is a *non zero sum* game, a game nobody ultimately has to lose. God calls to all, restrains none, and will accept all who come.

For the few who decide to take their own break from gaming (or whatever else it might be that ails you), let us conclude with a map of the way along the narrow path and a few warnings about pitfalls you may encounter, just in case you meet with some of the same obstacles I did. Let me also offer a few suggestions as to where to start on this journey.

First to the pitfalls. I had trouble regulating my sleep for quite some time after turning away from my sin. We are body and soul, and, as such, we are subject to both spiritual forces as well as chemical forces. Video games bring frequent emotional highs and lows, and it seems natural to suspect that this undoubtedly results in heightened levels of chemical activity in the brain. That being said, if you take a break from video games, to some degree, you have to allow that your body will go through a time of readjustment. There will be withdrawal symptoms.

Lest we think this somehow extraordinary or jump to extreme comparisons with heavy substance abuse, this is true of abstaining from any kind of perpetual sin, not just exorbitant video games. It is the nature of sin in general to excite and entice fallen man. Of course stealing gives us some sort of chemical high. Of course lying gives us a chemical high;

that's the theoretical basis for lie detector tests.[77] And on and on we could go. So whatever your idol might be, when you turn from it, you should expect to feel like your joy has been snatched from you, and the sin in you, along with your own body, will both want to return to things as they were. As we sin, we train our bodies to love sin, and when we stop giving in, we're certainly going to feel it for a time. The Bible anticipates this, as we have seen in many examples already—a season of sadness follows repentance from sin, which eventually gives way to renewed joy.

There may be some truth to the popular saying that "it takes twenty-one days to form a habit." For me, it was about three weeks before I could say I had a reasonably good day again. Twenty-one days might simply be how long your body takes to do a sort of chemical reset. It seems natural to suspect that our minds are adaptable to our life situations, that soldiers fighting wars, for instance, have different chemical needs than under-stimulated elderly people. Since gaming simulates exciting life situations in a very immersive way, the gamer's brain no doubt produces tons of chemicals, so it should be no surprise that cutting out a significant part of your regular routine will initiate a process of chemical re-balancing. This time of sorrow should not surprise us. God designed it to be this way, and the Bible expects that this will be the case. This was designed by God for our spiritual good. There will be a time of repenting from sin, of sorrow for what we have done and what we are, of being flooded with all sorts of negative emotions. This is not just a shallow chemistry experiment; it has a God-given purpose. The struggles of our cushy civilization are utterly trivial compared to the trials Paul experienced, but the purpose is the same:

> *For we were so utterly burdened beyond our strength that we despaired of life itself. Indeed, we felt that we had received the*

77 It is of interest to note that a lie detector test notes physical stress that comes about as a result of lying, whereas telling the truth results in no physical stress.

> *sentence of death. But that was to make us rely not on ourselves but on God who raises the dead. (2 Cor 1.9)*

To make himself central in our lives, God must make us see how utterly lost we are without him. We must recognize we have no hope apart from his grace. Consider the beatitudes. The word "blessed" doesn't mean much to us really. It sounds like a generic spiritual word, devoid of real content, but it is not. It has often been translated as "very happy" or "how happy!", since it certainly carries that connotation. It also carries a sense of flourishing or blooming. A person who is "blessed" is both happy and successful because God has shown favor (or grace) to them. Jesus measured this happy success in strange ways:

> *And he opened his mouth and taught them, saying:*
> *"Blessed are the poor in spirit, for theirs is the kingdom of heaven.*
> *"Blessed are those who mourn, for they shall be comforted.*
> *"Blessed are the meek, for they shall inherit the earth.*
> *"Blessed are those who hunger and thirst for righteousness, for they shall be satisfied." (Mt 5.2-6)*

Jesus always had a great love for paradoxes. Here he told us to recognize that it is the person who accounts himself spiritually impoverished who has, in truth, become wealthy on account of the gospel. Only those who recognize themselves as lowly sinners can be accounted righteous before God. Those who are weak in themselves become strong in him. The ones who mourn over their sin will be comforted by his grace. We mourn over our sin at our conversion, certainly, but this is also true of the Christian life in general. Repentance is a way of life for the Christian, and repentance always comes with some measure of sorrow and regret. In order to be blessed by God, we must rely upon God as we fight against our worldly desires. If you want to "be satisfied," according to Jesus, the key is to "hunger and thirst for righteousness." In short, if you turn away from the life of worldly, deceitful desires, you will find true satisfaction—true blessedness—in him, but only after a time of sorrow.

There were many days early on where I had very little joy; I appealed to God all day long to be true to his promises and to do in me what he had promised. For me, the first few weeks were mostly miserable, the next few were hit and miss, and, all totaled, it was close to two months before I felt normal again. Now that it is all said and done, I require at least an hour more sleep each night. I can't exactly explain why that is; I really don't know how it all works; I can only tell you that has been my experience. If you find yourself in a similar situation, you might consider resigning yourself to going to bed a couple of hours earlier than normal for a few weeks. God made sleep; sleep is good. You'll be sleeping for the sake of righteousness, and so be grateful to God for good and long and restful sleep.

Let me also offer a few suggestions as to how to begin this new journey, should you decide to take this path. First of all, you cannot expect that true happiness will come apart from the regular means (or methods) God has given us to draw near to him. Indeed, it will not. This is of paramount importance. Many waste a lifetime hoping to find a secret key to unlock the Bible and be miraculously transformed into better Christians. I am not very wise, but I am wise enough to know there is no secret key. Looking for a secret key to unlock the Bible is like looking for the secret key to becoming an Olympic swimmer that doesn't involve swimming. The Bible doesn't prescribe secret codes or keys; it only prescribes a lot of hard work—consistent diligence, strenuous effort, and patient perseverance. Spiritual health, like physical health, only comes through nourishment and exercise. No one became a mature Christian merely by chance or good fortune. A mature Christian is a disciplined Christian. There is no such thing as a mature, undisciplined Christian. This may all sound dreadful, I understand, but you must understand if you are consistent for a time, what was once dread will become your greatest delight. You will have discovered a better way on a narrow path.

The culture urges "moderation in everything," but you must ignore that and pursue God wholly. The notion that it's good to be a moderate Christian is a lie constructed by a world which tolerates us only insofar as we don't take the business of righteousness too seriously. Given all that has been said, it follows that a moderate Christian can only expect a moderate amount of happiness in God. Pursue the Christian life wholeheartedly. Pursue righteousness with everything in you. That is the true path to blessedness.

Was Jesus a man of spiritual moderation? No, Jesus was dead serious, a man on a mission, and he never lost sight of his mission, not even for a moment. He endured the cross "for the joy that was set before him" (Heb 12.2). The suffering before him was temporary, followed by an infinity of unending glory. Through suffering, he redeemed for himself a people (Tit 2.14).

Were the apostles men of moderation? Of course not. They fought as hard as they could for as long as they could. They were certain God had come to earth, was crucified for their sins, had risen from the dead, had ascended into the clouds, would come again soon, and would give the crown of life to the one who is faithful, even unto death (Rev 2.10). They learned the secret of godly self-interest for they found that their love of self, love of God, and love of others conjoined perfectly in the pursuit of spreading their Savior's message through the world. Even their persecution was something to rejoice over (Acts 5.41), for their cuts and bruises looked to them like everlasting glory. They fought so strenuously against the world that finally the world would have them no longer—Andrew crucified, Philip crucified, Bartholomew crucified, Peter crucified upside down, Steven stoned, James stoned, the other James killed with a sword, Mark dragged by horses through the streets, Paul beheaded.[78] Here are men who knew what it was to be like Christ—to be Christians! They

78 Church history tells us that all but one apostle—John—was martyred, and there is at least one ancient account indicating that John also underwent torture.

lived like him and they died like him. "Always give yourselves fully to the work of the Lord," said Paul, "because you know that your labor in the Lord is not in vain" (1 Cor 15.58).

Don't be content to sneak in the back door of heaven—that's the lie of worldly and lazy Christians. They say, "I'll be content to wash the floors just inside the gate," but notice what they've done there—they've tried to blur the line between humility and laziness to appease their aching consciences. No, that is not the path for you; you must fight furiously for the front row. Does Jesus desire mediocrity or excellence? Moderate worship or abundant and overflowing worship? Expose every lie in the world through every means you can think of. Why give him only part when you can give him the whole and thereby find the greatest happiness in him, the most glory, the largest capacity to love him more, both now and forever? Think of how much you will thank yourself later, when this momentary warring is over. We must violently struggle against our sin "so that when he appears we may have confidence and not shrink from him in shame at his coming" (1 Jn 2.28). Imagine that at the day of your death, if you are Christian, you will become 1000 times the Christian you were on that day. Now the least of Christians will be something remarkable for sure, but imagine what the greatest of Christians will be! Now the formula is make-believe, but the principle is true. Pleasant indeed will be those words: "Well done, good and faithful servant. You have been faithful over a little; I will set you over much. Enter into the joy of your master" (Mt 25.23).

To do this, you will need to become well acquainted with those things God uses to make us better Christians, the means of sanctifying grace. The Bible and prayer are paramount, but also important are reading other Christian books, listening to preaching, fasting, participating in God's sacraments (communion and baptism), regular church attendance, regular giving, and regular, quality fellowship with other Christians. There are, no doubt, dozens of others you will discover along the way. Christian service, in love, brings our joy to its highest fulfillment.

None of this comes naturally to us. You will wake up each morning finding that while you slept your heart has grown cold and your inclination is toward sin and against God. As Watson noted, "It is sad that our hearts should be so dead to heavenly things, and like a sponge to suck in earthly things."[79] Many days you will not feel like praying, but you must. Many days you will not feel inclined to read your Bible, but you must. Consider what you have before you! Listen to the words of John Wesley:

> *I have thought; I am a creature of a day, passing through life as an arrow through the air. I am a spirit come from God, and returning to God: just hovering over the great gulf; till, a few moments hence, I am no more seen; I drop into an unchangeable eternity! I want to know one thing—the way to heaven; how to land safe on that happy shore. God Himself has condescended to teach the way; for this very end He came from heaven. He hath written it down in a book. O give me that book! At any price, give me the book of God!* [80]

The bottom line is that you have to get the word of God in you, and you have to do it early and often and in many different ways. You will need good, regular habits to make any progress. There are many good books on disciplining yourself as a Christian which can help. I enjoyed *When I Don't Desire God: How to Fight for Joy* by John Piper, in which he argues "the fight for joy is the fight to see and believe Christ more to be desired than the promises of sin."

Every Christian life is to be a life of study. Whatever else you might be, you must always be a student, always a disciple under the great Master! There is no other way; God changes our hearts only through our minds. Words go in through the ears and eyes, they are processed by the

---

79 Thomas Watson, *The Art of Divine Contentment* (Grand Rapids, MI: Soli Deo Gloria Publications, 2011), 98.

80 John Wesley. Quoted in John Piper, *When I Don't Desire God: How to Fight for Joy* (Wheaton, IL: Crossway Books, 2004), 114.

mind, and only then can they begin to affect the heart. The heart cannot be changed apart from regular study. "The word must not only fall as dew that wets the leaf, but as rain which soaks to the root of the tree and makes it fruitful."[81] Reading, memorizing, studying—all of these have a transforming effect on us. Piper's words are important, perhaps even understated:

> *One of the ways we can fight against the inclinations that lure us from the Word of God to computers or television or any other substitute pleasure is to remind ourselves often of the immeasurable and superior benefits of the Word of God in our lives. We must put the evidence before us that reading, pondering, memorizing, and studying the Bible will yield more joy in this life and the next than all the things that lure us from it. (97)*

After four to six hours of television each day, we are satisfied with four to six minutes with God. We have more leisure time than any civilization in the history of the world. We are surrounded by machines that do all of our work for us, both at work and at home, yet never has mankind claimed to be so strapped for time. What explanation can we offer other than we are slaves of entertainment? We are a culture burdened and spread thin by the demands of our hobbies. Understand that where you spend your time is where you worship. If the things you spend your time on do not make you a better Christian, then get rid of every one of them, at least temporarily, until you can return to them with thanksgiving in your heart for the God who made them all. The resources at our fingertips are astounding, but most people squander all of it. Up through the Renaissance, the price of a single book was comparable to one's annual income in most cases. Now they are mostly free, and the costliest ones are still cheaper than a restaurant meal. An endless

81 Thomas Watson, *The Art of Divine Contentment* (Grand Rapids, MI: Soli Deo Gloria Publications, 2011), 4.

selection of classic Christian literature is available online for free. There are also tens of thousands of sermons available online for free to stream or download.[82] Though not one of them is perfect, there are dozens of quality expositors of Scripture.

Here is another folly of ours. When approaching any subject in the world, if you want to understand that subject, you know you have to consult the experts. You want to be a chemist; read some books on chemistry. You want to be a doctor; read some books by the medical experts. Yet when it comes to Christianity for some reason—some very poorly conceived reason—people say, "You don't need other books; just use the Bible by itself." If you were to choose a doctor for yourself, would you choose the one who was professionally trained, had read the best books, and who had consulted the experts? Or would you prefer the one who had no training, had not consulted the experts, but had instead just spent a few hours studying a cadaver? It is the pinnacle of arrogance, the peak of human stupidity, to think you can do just as well on your own in understanding the Bible as you can by utilizing all of the men who came before you over the last twenty centuries, each one studying and standing on the shoulders of those before him, thereby seeing a wee bit further into the boundless perfection of Holy Scripture. I suspect no one alive today understands the Bible as much as men like John Owen and John Calvin. Why wouldn't you read them? It's foolish not to. Read them all; test everything against Scripture. Cherish what is true and let the rest fade from memory. If you investigate the life of the bumpkin who suggests that you should not read books about the Bible but only the Bible itself, you will very likely find they are a spiritual child, since they have disregarded a major, normal, ordinary source of Christian growth, thereby scorning Christ's church and his power in men's lives through the course of history. Should you investigate the life of the bumpkin, you

82 A countless number of sermons can be found at www.sermonaudio.com. I have enjoyed the relevant teaching of R.C. Sproul, Tim Keller, and John Piper, whose sermons and lectures can be found on their respective websites.

will likely find that, not only does he not read the extra-biblical books, he doesn't read his Bible either. Every man is flawed, but that's not to say we should disregard the theological experts—no more than we would disregard the medical experts. The Spirit will teach us all things, it is true (cf. Jn 14.26[83]), but is that God's way of telling us we should sit back, do nothing, and wait to be filled with insight? No, the meaning is that the Spirit will guide Christ's sheep in the right path and keep us from deadly errors when we utilize the normal means, including extra-biblical Christian literature. History has already filtered out most of the lousy books for you; what remains is the cream of the crop; *tolle lege*, "take up and read."[84] Understanding God better always means loving him more, never less.[85]

Find a copy of Joel Beeke's *Readers Guide to Reformed Literature* in which Beeke recommends the best books available on nearly every biblical topic.[86] He frequently points out which books are best for beginners, which ones are the most practical, which ones are tough reading, etc. I have never been disappointed with following his recommendations. Again, many of his recommendations are free to download online. Start with those things you understand the least, because explosive learning often leads to faster running. Do not avoid anything for fear that it will change you; those are the books you need the most; read those first. If all of the books on a particular subject seem lousy, set about writing your own. If you spend twenty years researching and writing and

83 It should be remembered, also, that Jesus was addressing the apostles here, and primarily meant that the Spirit would remind them of everything he said in order to write the inspired books of the Bible.

84 Augustine, *Great Books of the Western World*, vol. 18, *The Confessions* (Chicago: Encyclopedia Britannica, 1993).

85 In the short bibliography at the end of the book, I have noted some books relevant to happiness and the Christian life, which could also be a good place to start.

86 Joel R. Beeke, *A Reader's Guide to Reformed Literature: An Annotated Bibliography of Reformed Theology* (Grand Rapids, MI: Reformation Heritage Books, 1999). Available at www.heritagebooks.org.

then die before it is finished, so be it. God rewards based on effort and intent more than on the actual result. The result is up to him; that is mostly outside of your control. Therefore, worry only about your own heart and motives each day. It will have been time well spent in worship, and you will have an eternity to finish your masterpiece later.[87] Your life does not end at your death; it continues forever—you yourself continue forever. Whether it be writing a book, or private journaling, or maintaining a blog, writing is another useful means of recognizing and breaking addictive patterns. It is another way God uses to help us understand him better, where understanding him better always causes us to love him more and to fight harder for him in every area.

Over time the transforming of your mind through the regular means that God has provided will begin to overflow in love. As you begin to see more clearly that Christ is in other Christians, your love for them will naturally abound. As your love for Christ grows, so too will your love for other Christians, since you will understand more clearly that the Spirit of Christ dwells in them. You are doing well when you see Christ in them, as much as you see them. I found that when I was wasting my time, I considered my time to be of immense value and kept it all to myself, but now that I am wasting much less, I give it away much more freely. Sometimes it even feels like the more time I give away, the more I have. The Lord knows how to make something out of nothing.

You must also surround yourself with other Christians. This will help anchor you in the truth. "Whoever isolates himself seeks his own desire; he breaks out against all sound judgment" (Pr 18.1). Start a Bible study or a book study with a friend or two. Nothing sharpens a person's mind like conversation and healthy debate. One of the most significant periods of spiritual growth in my own life came while I was meeting with

---

87 Randy Alcorn's book on Heaven, by the same name (see the bibliography), is commendable and dispels the notion that heaven is something like an endless Sunday school lesson. I agree with Alcorn that all human culture, including the writing of books, will continue on the New Earth.

friends to talk about books once a week at Denny's. We started with a plate of *Moons Over My Hammy* and Francis Schaeffer's thoughtful little book, *How Shall We Then Live?*

As your interest in God grows, you will not be able to restrain yourself from telling others what God has done for you. Witnessing to non-Christians will no longer be the awkward and dreaded endeavor it once was. No, the more you are conformed to Christ, the harder it will be to restrain yourself from talking about Christ. Many churches focus on evangelism to the neglect of Christian sanctification. Their members may be zealous to tell others of the gospel, but often they are intellectually and spiritually emaciated Christians, barely capable of explaining what the gospel is. This is backwards; first you must feed the sheep. Then their witnessing will come naturally, and their lifestyle itself will be a testimony to others. Your words are the natural overflow of the content of your heart. Fill up your heart and the words will come naturally.

Love overflows in countless ways, and not everyone is the same. Everyone is different and there is a place for each of us. There are many organs in the body, but still the body works together as a single, unified whole (Rom 12.4). Follow your talents and your joy in prayer and God will direct you in the right way, and you will find your proper role within Christ's church. The harvest is plentiful, but the laborers are few (Mt 9.37). There is more than enough work for everyone. Set your sights on the highest goal you think you can achieve and then a little higher, "for it is God who works in you, both to will and to work for his good pleasure" (Phil 2.13). Some will excel in acts of mercy. True religion, said James, is to visit widows and orphans (1.27).[88] Some will serve; some will lead; some will talk and teach; some will sit quietly and listen to the hurting and broken. Some will break their backs through hard labor for others and be rewarded greatly. Some will sit and study and write and

88 People who say you don't need "religion" have clearly missed the fact that the Bible refers to itself explicitly as a "religion."

hope that Christ would be pleased to use their writing, however feeble and however flawed, to further his kingdom. Some will avoid all liberties for Christ; some will partake of all liberties for Christ (Rom 14.6). The body of Christ is vast. If you search, you will find your place within it. The more gifts God has blessed you with, the more will be required of you (Lk 12.48). If you don't have many gifts, don't be discouraged, but consider the offering of the widow:

> *Jesus sat down opposite the place where the offerings were put and watched the crowd putting their money into the temple treasury. Many rich people threw in large amounts. But a poor widow came and put in two very small copper coins, worth only a few cents. Calling his disciples to him, Jesus said, "Truly I tell you, this poor widow has put more into the treasury than all the others. They all gave out of their wealth; but she, out of her poverty, put in everything—all she had to live on." (Mk 12.41–44)*

Consider also some old Puritan wisdom:

> *Now you may be faithful in little as well as others are in more, by going on and working your day's labor; when you get but a couple of shillings to maintain your family, you may be as faithful in this as those who rule a kingdom. God looks to a man's faithfulness, and you may have all as great a reward for your faithfulness who are a poor servant in the kitchen all the day, as another who sits upon the throne all day. As great a crown of glory you may have at the day of judgment, as a king who sits upon the throne, who has ruled for God upon his throne....the Lord does not so much look at the work that is done, as at the faithfulness of our hearts in doing it...I cannot come to be as rich a man and as honorable as others; but I may be as faithful as any other man.*[89]

89 Jeremiah Burroughs, *The Rare Jewel of Christian Contentment* (1648; repr.,

Above all, delight in your labor! It is one of the greatest lies that ever snuck into the church of Christ that God values a thing more when I don't enjoy it. This is one of Satan's greatest pranks on us. We believe God wants unfortunate and unhappy sacrifice from us, but it is not so. The sacrifice God wants is the "sacrifice of thanksgiving" (cf. Ps 116.17). Thanksgiving and praise make our acts valuable to God:

> *...contentment not only makes our duties lively and agile, but acceptable. It is this that puts beauty and worth into them, for contentment settles the soul. When milk is always stirring, you can make nothing of it, but let it settle awhile and then it turns to cream. In the same way, when the heart is overly stirred with disquiet and discontent, you can make nothing of those duties. How thin, how flat, how dull are they! But when the heart is once settled by holy contentment, now there is some worth in our duties, now they turn to cream.* [90]

Friends, what we will be has not yet been made known (1 Jn 3.2), but we know we have been adopted (Eph 1.5) into the divine nature (2 Pet 1.4), so we are, as it were, the true children of God (Gal 3.26), adopted members of the divine family. We are co-heirs with Christ (Rom 8.17), and our Father will give to us what he will give to his only begotten and True Son—his very best—and he will withhold nothing. Therefore, I think it safe to say that when the omniscient, omnipotent, omnipresent, all-seeing, all-wise, preeminent, absolute, eternal Yahweh determines to express his love, to give his children the best day of their eternal lives, every day, he succeeds in ways that are infinitely exalted above anything of which we could conceive. As it is written, "Eye hath not seen, nor ear heard, neither have entered into the heart of man, the things which

---

Carlisle, PA: The Banner of Truth Trust, 2009), 199.

90 Thomas Watson, *The Art of Divine Contentment* (Grand Rapids, MI: Soli Deo Gloria Publications, 2011), 62.

God hath prepared for them that love him" (1 Cor 2.9 KJV).[91] Therefore, "Rejoice always, pray without ceasing, give thanks in all circumstances; for this is the will of God in Christ Jesus for you" (1 Thes 5.16-18).

We all feel in the core of our being the unmistakable suspicion that we were made for something great, something more. There is a longing inside that cannot be quelled. Don't try to ignore it, but rather embrace the fact that our calling—your calling—is the highest conceivable calling imaginable—to glorify God by enjoying him forever. You have been called to worship the Most High in a way only you can. You have been called to fulfill a particular role within God's grand design, a role which only you can perfectly and uniquely fulfill.

Our culture is unwell, and we are unwell alongside it. Never has man been so well-connected and yet so completely isolated. We are surrounded with "friends" and "followers" and yet we are viscerally lonely. We are always bickering but committed to nothing. Here, in Christ, is a true family that never dissolves or has to choose between love of self or love of another, for they are one and the same; Christ is in all and through all. Here is a revolution worth staging, a "good warfare" (1 Tim 1.18) worth fighting. There is no greater cause than this one. All other causes combined are as nothing in comparison with this one. Here is truth unchanging, eternal, absolute, and final. Here is a Savior wanting to bless you, wanting to increase your joy, wanting to trade his strength for your weakness, his righteousness for your sin. He is always recruiting and never refuses any who seek him (Jn 6.37).

Put away childish things (1 Cor 13.11). Keep yourselves from idols (1 Jn 5.21). "No soldier gets entangled in civilian pursuits, since his aim is to please the one who enlisted him" (2 Tim 2.4). Trade in your virtual warfare for the true warfare, your virtual sword and shield for the true sword and shield of faith (Eph 6.13-20). The battle begins within you and

---

91 In context, this verse is referencing the appearance of Jesus, although Paul makes some citations here from Isaiah, in which Isaiah seems to be referring to heaven, so I trust this usage is fair.

then naturally moves outward. Take courage, fear nothing, the outcome is certain; in Christ we are already conquerors—no—more than conquerors (Rom 8.37).

WORKS CITED

Alcorn, Randy. Heaven. N/A: Tyndale House Publishers. 2004.

Aquinas. *Great Books of the Western World.* Vol 17: The Summa Theologica. Chicago, IL: Encyclopedia Britannica. 1993.

Augustine of Hippo. *The Confessions.* Chicago, IL: Encyclopedia Britannica. 1993.

Beeke, Joel R. *A Reader's Guide to Reformed Literature: An Annotated Bibliography of Reformed Theology.* Grand Rapids, MI: Reformation Heritage Books. 1999.

Burroughs, Jeremiah. *The Rare Jewel of Christian Contentment.* 1648. Reprint, Carlisle, PA: The Banner of Truth Trust. 2009.

Charry, Ellen T. *God and the Art of Happiness.* Grand Rapids, MI: Wm. B. Eerdmans Publishing Co. 2010.

Schroeder, Stan. "Diablo 3 is the fastest selling PC game in history." *Mashable Entertainment.* May 23, 2012. http://mashable.com/2012/05/23/diablo-3-fastest-selling/

Dougherty, T. *Evolution Evolves: A Presuppositional Argument Against Naturalism.* Cuyahoga Falls, OH: Sledge Press. 2014.

Dougherty, T. *The Secret of Sacrificial Self-Service: Discovering the Spiritual Incentives of Christian Hedonism.* Sledge Press. 2021.

Dr. Seuss. *The Cat in the Hat.* New York, NY: Random House. 1957.

Durant, Will. *The Story of Civilization: Part 3: Caesar and Christ.* New York, NY: Simon and Schuster. 1944.

Morin, Richard. "Famous for 15 Minutes." *Washington Post*. August 28, 2000. http://www.washingtonpost.com/wp-srv/politics/polls/wat/archive/wat082800.htm

Fight Club. DVD. Directed by David Fincher. 20th Century Fox. 1999.

Hendriksen, William. *New Testament Commentary: Romans.* Grand Rapids, MI. 2004.

"If All of Work Were Gamified." Bloomberg Businessweek. *Harvard Business Review.* May 24, 2011.

http://www.businessweek.com/managing/content/may2011/ca20110524_211203.htm

Kierkegaard, Søren. *The Sickness Unto Death*. Princeton, NJ: Princeton University Press. 1941.

Lewis, C. S. *The Screwtape Letters.* New York, NY: HarperCollins. 2001.

Lloyd-Jones, D. Martyn. *Spiritual Depression: It's Causes and Cure.* Grand Rapids, MI: Wm. B. Eerdmans. 1965.

Pipa, Joseph A., Jr. *The Lord's Day*. Geanies House, Fearn, Ross-shire IV201TW, Great Britain: Christian Focus. 2008.

Piper, John. *Desiring God: Meditations of a Christian Hedonist.* Portland, OR: Multnomah. 1986.

----. *When I Don't Desire God: How to Fight for Joy.* Wheaton, IL: Crossway Books. 2004.

Sheldon, Henry C. History of Christian Doctrine, 2 volumes. New York: Harper & Brothers Publishers. 1895.

Watson, Thomas. *The Art of Divine Contentment.* 1653. Reprint, Grand Rapids, MI: Soli Deo Gloria Publications. 2011.

Whitney, Donald S. *Spiritual Disciplines for the Christian Life.* Colorado Springs, CO: Navpress. 1991.

Winter, Richard. *Still Bored in a Culture of Entertainment.* Downer Grove, IL. Intervarsity Press. 2002.

Youssef, Michael. *Divine Discontent.* Colorado Springs, CO: Waterbrook Press. 2004.

www.ingramcontent.com/pod-product-compliance
Lightning Source LLC
LaVergne TN
LVHW010924110826
845149LV00013B/2473

* 9 7 8 0 9 9 0 8 0 0 8 4 2 *